Joyce's Waking Women

Joyce's Waking Women

An Introduction to *Finnegans Wake*

SHELDON BRIVIC

The University of Wisconsin Press

The University of Wisconsin Press
114 North Murray Street
Madison, Wisconsin 53715

3 Henrietta Street
London WC2E 8LU, England

Library of Congress Cataloging-in-Publication Data
Brivic, Sheldon, 1943–
Joyce's waking women: an introduction to Finnegans wake /
Sheldon Brivic.
176 p.   cm.
Includes bibliographical references and index.
ISBN 0-299-14800-9.   ISBN 0-299-14804-1 (pbk.)
1. Joyce, James, 1882–1941. Finnegans wake. 2. Feminism and
literature—Ireland—History—20th century. 3. Women and
literature—Ireland—History—20th century. 4. Joyce, James,
1882–1941—Characters—Women. 5. Ireland—In literature.
I. Title.
PR6019.09F563   1995
823'.912—dc20   95-6475

For Anna Glogover Brivic
Awake, awake, utter a song

Contents

Preface   ix

Abbreviations   xiii

1. Introduction: Joyce toward Women   3

2. Two Songs   26

3. The Voice of the River   35

4. Afric Anna: Joyce's Multiracial Heroine   54

5. Going to the Chapel   68

6. The Terror and Pity of Love: ALP's Soliloquy   81

7. A Leap Past: ALP between Deaths   113

8. Conclusion: Annual Increments   132

Notes   139

Works Cited   145

Index   155

Preface

My previous book, *The Veil of Signs*, was a hard one to write; this one was easy. Though I was aware of the difficulties involved in reading *Finnegans Wake* and in writing as a man about feminist issues, I found that both of my main subjects gave me abundant access to beauty. Having forged some Lacanian ideas in the last book, I enjoyed applying and modifying them here.

Though I first read the *Wake* in 1965–67, it was not until many years later that I realized that Joyce was right about this being his finest work. The length of time that it takes to see the value of the *Wake* is one of the main problems that I address here. The Anglophone literary accomplishment of the century probably cannot be read well in one course. Months of reading tend to derail the sense of continuity most books provide. Parts of the *Wake* are harder to appreciate than others, and some of the less exciting parts appear in chapters 2 to 4 near the beginning (I examine chapter 4 in *The Veil of Signs*). Yet selected passages, dazzling and uproarious, can get the book's greatness across quickly.

The solution I opt for here is to violate the taboo against disintegrating the work's organic wholeness. After all, parts of the *Wake* were first published as booklets; and several recent critics have favored extracting elements from their contexts (Bishop 305–16) or seeing the book as a hypertext, to be read in various orders (Riquelme 10–17). I hope to get readers involved in a few of the book's best parts with the help of vital contemporary ideas. I use the *Wake*'s sexual frankness and irreverence, but I try to make the most use of its concern for humanity, and for the parts of humanity that have been held under. This concern provides the greatest beauty. I approach what has been held under through psychoanalysis, hoping to describe the maladjustments of society and history through the system that explains irrational motivation.

My focus on the question of women means that I usually do not try to cover every level of meaning in a given unit of the text. Though I occasionally do discuss a range of possible interpretations for a phrase, mostly I emphasize levels that contribute to gender issues and leave out important interpretations available in standard sources. This would seem to be a way in which feminism takes precedence over introduction, but the book would not serve its purpose of getting the reader into the *Wake* quickly if its length were not controlled.

Actually, this book started as a study of Anna Livia Plurabelle, and when I mentioned that I would focus on two sections about her, Margot Norris suggested that this might make a good introduction to the *Wake*. I expected to like working on the *Wake*, but was surprised at how much feminism appeals to me: it is the appeal of the opposite. A dozen years ago, while reading *Housekeeping*, by Marilynne Robinson, I grew aware that I could be enchanted by a world of women in which men were absent. Perhaps this was because I had often found manhood onerous, but it certainly was because the peace of a world without men is something I'll never see. Like Milton's Satan, I carry hell within myself. Fortunately, I have been taking lessons on the connection between women and peace for thirty-three years from my wife, Barbara.

I organized panels on feminism in the *Wake*, on Anna Livia, and on her racial features at the MLA Convention in New York in 1992, the California Joyce Conference at Irvine in 1993, and the Seville Joyce Symposium in 1994. Members of these groups included Berni Benstock, Marilyn Brownstein, Kim Devlin, Marian Eide, Lynda Hill, Barbara Lonnquist, Margot Norris, and Aïda Yared. I am grateful to all of them for their help: most of them read parts of the manuscript and commented. I was also helped by a paper Vicki Mahaffey read on a panel on marriage in Joyce that I led in Dublin in 1992.

My greatest debt is to Berni, who read the whole MS and commented profusely. He pointed out that the anagram joining HCE and ALP was not my discovery. The passing of this incredibly productive man was a great loss to Joyce studies that will be offset by the hundreds of Joyceans he developed personally with his kindness.

I would like to thank Temple University for a study leave that helped me to complete this project. Among my colleagues, Dick Beckman's brilliant devotion to the *Wake* played a big role in making me a *Wake* scholar, Lynda Hill added sophistication to my fourth chapter, Steve Cole gave me good advice in the early planning stages, and Paula Robison was amused.

Much of my sixth chapter appeared in a somewhat different form in *James Joyce Quarterly*, and its editor, Robert Spoo, helped get this book under way by asking me to edit a special issue on Joyce, Lacan, and gender.

Beckman's Philadelphia Ideal Insomniacs reads about two-thirds of a page of the *Wake* every two weeks. Members have included David Borodin, Martha Davis, Mort Levitt, Barbara Lonnquist, Tim Martin, Mike O'Shea, and Steve Steinhof. They all provided ideas and support. Dick and I have been doing this for fifteen years.

In 1980 someone visited our group twice and identified a number of African words on a page we were doing. He planted in me a feeling that a lot of African material was to be found in the *Wake*. In 1994, after I had finished my MS, I told Patrick McCarthy that I had written a chapter arguing that ALP was predominantly African, and he mentioned that Karl Reisman had been working on African elements in the *Wake* for years. I contacted him and found that he was the one who had visited us in 1980. He is close to completing a book, "White Man's Wake," about African materials, languages, and readings in the *Wake*. Reisman says that his findings and mine do not overlap significantly, but reinforce each other.

I am also grateful to Garry Leonard, who clarified my understanding of Lacan and his relation to women; to Colleen Lamos, who offered information on feminist theory; to David Bloom, who provided sharp criticism; to William Melvin Kelley and Toni Morrison, who sent information on Africa; and to Wim Van Mierlo, who sent Margaret Maitland's life of Saint Martin. Finally, Barbara Brivic read the manuscript and made many helpful corrections and suggestions.

Abbreviations

The following abbreviations refer to the corresponding works of Joyce and to Ellmann's biography. Bibliographic data on these works are given in my Works Cited.

CW	*Critical Writings*
D	*Dubliners*
E	*Exiles*
FW	*Finnegans Wake*. References to the *Wake* will give the page number, a period, and the line number.
JJ	Richard Ellmann, *James Joyce*
JJA	*The James Joyce Archive*. See Note at the beginning of Works Cited.
Letters I, II	*Letters of James Joyce*, Vols. I and II
P	*Case Studies in Contemporary Criticism: A Portrait of the Artist as a Young Man*
SL	*Selected Letters of James Joyce*
U	*Ulysses*. References to *Ulysses* will give the episode number, a period, and the line number.

Joyce's Waking Women

1

Introduction

Joyce toward Women

Ibsen's knowledge of humanity is nowhere more obvious than in his portrayal of women. He amazes one by his painful introspection; he seems to know them better than they know themselves. Indeed, if one may say so of an eminently virile man, there is a curious admixture of the woman in his nature. His marvellous accuracy, his faint traces of femininity, his delicacy of swift touch, are perhaps attributable to this admixture.

—Joyce, "Ibsen's New Drama" (1900)

ROUNDING UP LOST HISTEREVE

Finnegans Wake, Joyce's most advanced work, not only explores the minds of women incisively, as one would expect from the man who gave birth to Molly Bloom, but contains sharp and systematic expressions of radical feminist insight. Many critics have seen deep sympathy for the cause of women in the *Wake*, including Shari Benstock, John Bishop, Kim Devlin, Suzette Henke, Margot Norris, Susan Shaw Sailer, and Bonnie Kime Scott (see Works Cited). Yet the strength of the *Wake*'s feminism has not been fully recognized, partly because of the obscurity of the text and partly because of Joyce's mixed record with regard to women.

As an egotistical man who grew up in Victorian Ireland, Joyce had serious limits in his views of women; but he worked against those limits so remarkably that, like his early master Ibsen, he deserves a place in the history of feminism. Perhaps he should be put in a line of male feminists whose contributions must be weighed against the ambiguity of their positions as men, including several figures I will refer to: Sophocles, John Webster, John Stuart Mill, and Jacques Lacan.

One reason the intensity of Joyce's feminism has not been seen is

3

that only recently, through such thinkers as Lacan and Luce Irigaray, has feminism developed theories that correspond to some of his more advanced ideas on the relation of women to language and society. I do not claim that these theories constitute the correct version of feminism—in fact Lacan and Irigaray often disagree—but they are active current theories and I will try to show ways in which they reveal valuable understanding of the genders.[1] It may be debated whether Lacan is a feminist thinker, for he often seems attached to masculine values; but a number of feminists, such as Juliet Mitchell and Elizabeth Grosz, have argued that his very investment in the phallus gives his theory special power to critique the existing patriarchal social order (Grosz 142, 189). Grosz, who is quite critical of Lacan, says that his ideas on the formation of subject and gender are invaluable to feminists, but they must be supplemented and revised by thinkers who take women's points of view, such as Irigaray (Grosz 190). This is my aim.

In tracing feminist arguments through the *Wake*, I must consider that like any Wakean arguments, they are sporadic, and must be lent continuity if they are to be seen as purposive. The *Wake*, as Derek Attridge (10–23) shows, demonstrates that all purpose must be constructed. And the *Wake*'s deconstructive texture has an affinity with feminism in going against phallocentric authority. It pushes off from the solid land of realistic convention to float toward the feminine values I show building throughout the book.

Sailer (72–78, 199–201) argues that the incoherence of the *Wake* leads to the construction of a series of coherences and sees the movement through this series as representing woman's shifting discourse. Feminism, however, is not more developed in the text than Attridge's deconstruction or Bishop's sleep or history or the family or postcolonialism. The very fact that women take up only a small fraction of the book means that feminism is unlikely to be seen as a totalizing explanation. As a new theory of interpretation, it increases the productivity of the text, which would be curtailed by taking feminism as the key to the city. But insofar as I want to delineate the fierceness of the *Wake*'s feminism, I will have to emphasize some linear connections.

Richard Ellmann reports that Joyce remarked that "he conceived of his book as the dream of old Finn, lying in death beside the river Liffey. . . ." (*JJ* 544). The ancient Irish hero Finn being an archaic and powerful aspect of the male protagonist Humphrey Chimpden Earwicker (HCE), there is reason to see prominent among the meanings of the title *Finnegans Wake* the idea of the burial of the patriarchal principle itself. It will be reborn, but the construction of the book, which ends with a woman's voice, implies that the father can be reborn only by listening to the mother, who ends up saying disturbing things.

Shoshana Felman (72–120) says that Freud gave birth to psychoanalysis by feeling and trying to understand the opposition of one of his hysterics ("Irma") and of other women associated with her. Her resistance made him aware of the unconscious, of the division within himself. Joyce's continuing exploration of the feminine also aimed at an unknowable opposite that corresponded to what he had repressed, and Joyce's works all end by focusing on a woman's resistance.

In opposition to the male narrative of the *Wake* there is a female one. The female narrative is usually submerged, but always present in the gaps of male discourse. We can focus on its usual form by following Richard Pearce's (11, 21) procedure of looking for holes, gaps in the coherence of patriarchal discourse that reveal the interference of submerged voices. Moreover, the female narrative emerges forcefully at a number of climactic points, including the end. The male story enacts conflict and decline, but the female one may be seen as showing discovery and development that proceed through the disintegration of the discourse of patriarchal coherence. The noncoherence of every page of the *Wake* speaks for Anna Livia Plurabelle (ALP), whose letter is equated with the book. Her quest for self-integration proceeds through interaction with the male, but may ultimately pass beyond male mediation.

ALP, the mother-river of the *Wake*, who has often been called one of the great woman characters in literature, is unleashed along with a searching critique of the historical role of women. I will take a clause out of context to describe her, for the *Wake* is so constructed that its words are perpetually escaping from their contexts: "she rounded up lost histereve . . ." (*FW* 214.1). This line refers to Anna only insofar as she is identified with the situation of all women. She recovers their lost history, with reference to *hystera*, the Greek for womb, and to Eve. She has also, as my student Justin Coffin observed, waited perpetually on the eve of the time that the lost history of women could be written.

Anna is identified most with her daughter, Issy (Isabel or Isolt), and her servant Kate, who are both separate characters and versions of Anna, her youth and her age. Distinctions between characters in the *Wake* tend to dissolve. On her Kate side, Anna appears as Biddy the hen, who gathers from the field of conflict the litter that makes up the letter identified with the *Wake* itself. The pieces she gathers speak not for the winners of history, who get to speak for themselves, but for the defeated and suppressed. The letter has Anna's voice, so it speaks for women as the conquered and dispersed of history, the group most consistently obliged to be refugees from themselves. These fragments are the breakages or flaws in the campaign of patriarchal discourse to dominate both genders, so these breakages speak for women.

Irigaray says that because male standards have dominated civilization, women's thoughts and feelings—the range of women's imagery for which she uses the Lacanian term "imaginary"—have been cast out so that they are hard to recover: "But if the female imaginary were to deploy itself, if it could bring itself into play otherwise than as scraps, uncollected debris, would it represent itself, even so, in the form of *one* universe?" (30). Irigaray does not think that she wants women's knowledge drawn together into a unity, for that would give it phallocentric authority. The freedom represented by womanhood depends on its dispersal. This is a major reason why the *Wake*, as Anna's letter, should never be reducible to a single clear meaning. It should never equal itself, for that is a prime characteristic of the phallus (Lemaire 86).

Throughout his career Joyce attacked patriarchy with devastating psychological acuity and insisted on the actual conditions women were subject to. This is most obvious in *Dubliners*.[2] "Araby" shows how an adolescent boy avoids the reality of a girl he knows in order to project a fantasy about her. "Counterparts" and "Two Gallants" show men who abuse children and women respectively to support their masculinity. "Eveline" shows a woman obliterated by her position within a family, while "Clay" shows one obliterated by her position outside a family; and "A Painful Case" shows a woman driven to suicide because she falls in love with a man who is extremely rational. In "Grace" Mrs. Kernan finds "a wife's life . . . unbearable" (*D* 156).

Such observation of social reality is the first phase of feminism, as Elaine Showalter (181–85) indicates, the critique of patriarchy; the second phase is the expression of woman's lives and thoughts outside the masculine structures that have enclosed them. In *Ulysses* and the *Wake* Joyce contributed to the development of the concepts of feminine language and mentality by developing styles that broke down masculine logical structures and released feminine flow.

Such writing was later to be called *écriture féminine*, and though Dorothy Richardson and Virginia Woolf had been developing feminine writing since the teens, Joyce's experiments went further and directly inspired two of the leading thinkers of the *écriture féminine* movement, Hélène Cixous and Julia Kristeva.[3] Joyce also influenced Lacan and Jacques Derrida during their formative years, as they attest;[4] and therefore current developments linking feminism and poststructuralism may be considered partly as the blooming of seeds Joyce planted. Susan Stanford Friedman mentions another anglophone Parisian in this line: "Poststructuralist theory is, in the eyes of many, an extension into philosophy, psychoanalysis, and linguistics of what writers such as Gertrude Stein and Joyce forged in literary discourse" (3).

Of course, the theory of feminine writing is a controversial one. Showalter (192–93) says that there is no evidence that women use language differently than men. If women's language is identical to men's, then their mentality is also identical; yet there are different mindsets known as masculine and feminine, and the genders have been historically linked to them. So if there are situations in which the language of women slides more than that of men, this is not inherited, but caused by patriarchal society, which designates it as typical. Nevertheless, virtually all attempts to distinguish women's language from men's return to the same "Joycean" flowing features.

Social criticism and feminine writing may conflict when feminists disagree about whether to emphasize social or personal factors, but society and personality cause each other. Joyce's rich awareness of the interplay between culture and psyche allowed him to make social criticism and feminine writing work together. I can sketch this interaction through a quick glance at Molly Bloom. As James Van Dyck Card (38–54) has shown, Molly contradicts herself at every turn, to such an extent that whenever she takes a position on any issue, she soon takes the opposing one. Molly's shifting positions precisely fit a formula Irigaray urges women to cultivate: "Nothing is ever to be *posited* that is not also reversed and caught up again in the *supplementarity of this reversal*" (79–80). Such emphasis on change pulsates through innovative techniques in "Penelope" like shifting pronoun references and syntax and jumping rapidly from one framework or imagined scene to another. But this experimental texture reflects Molly's political situation as a woman. Her contradictions delineate the traditional female condition, adding up to an inability to maintain a consistent subject position, to be responsible. Irigaray eschews the subject position in her desire to eradicate patriarchy, but within patriarchal society, Molly is devalued because of her inconstancy.

Molly condemns men, but depends on them for her identity. She affirms the virtues of women, but is in conflict with virtually every woman she knows because of the competitive system of exchange in which they are objects. She realizes that Leopold Bloom wants her to see Blazes Boylan, but cannot allow herself to see the extent to which she may be seeing Boylan for Bloom's sake. Wanting Bloom emotionally, but unable to accept him physically, she cannot recognize her responsibility for her alienation from him. Nor can she see how they are obstructed by their need to fit conventional gender roles: she cannot confront the way in which they actually relate to one another, with his passivity promoting her activity, which in turn stimulates his passivity.

In fact Molly's lack of self-possession or subjectivity is an instrument she uses to bind Bloom to her. The controlled male mind traditionally finds relaxation in the conditioned indefiniteness of the female mind. The free-floating mentality in which Bloom sustains Molly is the central object of his desire. His home would not be as cozy if she were fully rational and not compromised, just as she would not be as attractive to him if she were faithful. Yet Molly, as Kimberly Devlin ("Castration," "Pretending") points out, takes a step toward liberation insofar as she sees through her feminine drift and takes it as a masquerade.[5] Her ironic tone and her enjoyment of mental flow indicate a measure of self-possession, and she uses the indefiniteness of sex appeal to manipulate Bloom and other men. Thus, the shifting that is conditioned by society becomes a source of enjoyment and a tool to influence social arrangements, a self action—so that the political and the personal generate each other.

There is, however, a contradiction behind Joyce's insights because he is a male feminist. Whatever the value of his depiction of Molly's inconsistencies, there is something too snide in his enjoyment of her reversals. Even a man better at resisting adolescent sexism than Joyce has to see women's issues through his own interests. I give Joyce credit for recognizing his attraction toward debasing women, and focusing on the system that generated it. When Cranly asks Stephen in *Portrait* if he would deflower a virgin, Stephen asks, "is that not the ambition of most young gentlemen?" (*P* 213). And after a round of lustful thoughts, Stephen realizes, "His mind bred vermin" (*P* 202): he is corrupted by a debased society. So I will be following a Joycean procedure if I watch out for an undertow of masculine conditioning that may distort Joyce's most enlightened efforts.

His biggest blind spot was his dislike of intellectual women, which was especially lamentable since such women supported him throughout his career. There was some self-mockery in lines like "I hate women who know anything" (Maddox 207). Joyce felt that such women took on negative, abstract, pretentious features of male intelligence; and Irigaray's misgiving about unifying women's knowledge shows that a feminist may fear that highly rational women may become like men. Joyce's women usually know more than his men about how to live, and Devlin ("Romance Heroine," "Pretending") has shown that they make resourceful and clever choices among their limited options. But Joyce's anxiety about female talent fits a man who, as Lacan says of Joyce, identifies his art with his phallus (Aubert 41), and it overlaps with traditional attitudes used to keep women in their supposed place. We must see when and why Joyce's ideas tend to go wrong if we are to appreciate how right they often are, and similar things may be said of many feminists.

AIMING AT WOMEN

Joyce's works aim at women in at least four ways, making them both goal and target, but his leading aim is understanding. First, all of his major works end focused on the mind of a woman, and this is the goal of perception toward which each work moves. The exception seems to be *Portrait*, but on its last page Stephen Dedalus realizes that "all that I thought I thought and all that I felt I felt" about Emma Clery has been wrong, as if he were noticing that his sexism was imposed on him from outside. Then he writes that his mother prays that "I may learn in my own life and away from home and friends what the heart is and what it feels" (*P* 218). This line, her last before she appears as someone who has passed away, carries force as a scenario for *Ulysses*, the feminine knowledge that Stephen has to learn. At the end of "The Dead" Gretta Conroy sleeps while her husband thinks of her mind, but in *Exiles*, *Ulysses*, and the *Wake*, the man sleeps at the end, while the woman wakes. As Joyce's career progresses, he gets closer to the woman, and her waking grows more significant.

Second, Joyce's works were to a considerable extent, if not primarily, addressed to women. His writing began as a discourse to be read to his mother, who was the first audience for his early fiction, as his sister May records in a letter of 1916 (*Letters II* 383).[6] Mark Shechner (240) suggests that his work continued to be addressed to his mother after she died, and that he tried to recreate his maternal muse with Nora Barnacle. Joyce's persistence in trying to impress Nora with his mature work was remarkable in the face of her resistance. Brenda Maddox mentions that Nora "was more tolerant of *Work in Progress* than she had been of *Ulysses* and liked its musicality" (324); and the primary reader of the *Wake* in progress was Harriet Shaw Weaver, its patroness.

Mary Joyce, who had some fifteen children by an alcoholic, was for Joyce the great model of oppressed womanhood. In 29 August 1904 he wrote to Nora, "My mother was slowly killed, I think, by my father's ill treatment, by years of trouble, and by my cynical frankness of conduct. When I looked on her face as she lay in her coffin . . . I understood that I was looking on the face of a victim and I cursed the system which had made her a victim" (*Letters II* 48). This was the original person to whom his works were addressed.

In *Portrait*, Stephen commits himself to writing mainly for women as he looks at the ascendant class of Ireland outside Maple's Hotel: "How could he hit their conscience or how cast his shadow over the imaginations of their daughters, before their squires begat upon them, that they might breed a race less ignoble than their own?" (*P* 205). This passage suggests that when Joyce made ironic remarks about women, he usually felt that he was attacking the conventionality imposed on them. This does not justify his wisecracks, but it shows how they could coexist with better intentions. His ironies about women are matched by ironies about men, about himself, and about the things he believed in. See, for example, his savage treatment of himself as a low "sham" in the readable Shem chapter of the *Wake* (*FW* 169–95, known as I.7).[7] But Joyce had strong beliefs, and he indicated his commitment to feminism in a statement to Arthur Power around 1923, when he was beginning work on the *Wake*. Defending Ibsen, Joyce said that the purpose of *A Doll's House* "was the emancipation of women, which has caused the greatest revolution in our time in the most important relationship there is—that between men and women; the revolt of women against the idea that they are the mere instruments of men" (Power 35).

At the start of the "Oxen of the Sun" episode of *Ulysses*, which takes place at a maternity ward, a tangled narrative voice says that "by no exterior splendour is the prosperity of a nation more efficaciously asserted than by the measure of how far forward may have progressed the tribute of its solicitude for . . . proliferant continuance" (*U* 14.12–15). Having said that a nation should be evaluated by its care for motherhood, the text goes on to say that the ancient Celts, who admired all that was admirable, provided every possible means to make things easeful for childbearing women, and that this should be praised in a "prudent nation" (*U* 14.34–57). These sentiments are somewhat Victorian, they reduce women to vessels of birth, and they are ironic in relation to the actual misery of Irish mothers like Mary Joyce. Nevertheless, the passage does state that the highest civilization is the one that cares best for its women, and this seems to have been a principle of Joyce's.

Maddox (221) says that without lavish support from the radical feminist Weaver, Joyce would never have written the *Wake* as freely as he did, though Maddox is not sure this is a good thing. Bonnie Kime Scott says that Joyce sent samples and explanations of the *Wake* to Weaver so often that "she became the reader who wrote the book," and adds, "The mature and capable women who lived through *Finnegans Wake* with Joyce repeatedly suggest that this was a man who had grown beyond the limits of Stephen Dedalus" (*Joyce and Feminism* 97, 115). Biography, then, suggests reasons why Joyce, in creating Anna, would have had feminist ideas in mind. The critics I cited at the start, who saw a strong concern for women in the *Wake*, are part of an extensive stream. As early as 1957 Northrop Frye said of Anna's position in the *Wake*, "In Joyce the central figure is female because the containing form is ironic and cyclical" (263).

Margot Norris demonstrates in *Joyce's Web* (8–9, 18–21, 25) that Joyce carried out a continual process of self-criticism throughout his career, making his later texts comment on his earlier ones. She emphasizes that through this procedure he strengthened his social criticism and carried his feminism to new levels of understanding. Thus Norris shows why Joyce's internal development caused the *Wake* to include his toughest vision of women's point of view.

Anna emerges most fully in two short, relatively self-contained sections of the *Wake* that I focus on, the "Anna Livia Plurabelle" chapter (I.8) and the last fourteen pages of the book, which include Anna's letter and her soliloquy. These are generally regarded as two of the very best parts of the *Wake*, and are parallel to each other.[8] Yet they represent different phases of Joyce's career, appearing at the beginning and the end of the sixteen-year composition of Joyce's main work. "ALP" was substantially written from 1923 to 1928, though there were later revisions, while the soliloquy was written in 1938 (*JJ* 563 794–95, 711), and is more intense in its feminism. To introduce my readings of these sections, I will first discuss Joyce's relation to feminist theory and then examine a pair of motifs to indicate some structural principles of the *Wake* and to show how these principles are related to the concept of woman's language and the theme of her awakening.

Some strengths and weaknesses of Joyce's feminism may be seen by starting with a rousing quote from Issy, who is both ALP's daughter and her youth, identities being permeable in the *Wake*. Issy speaks as one who has been trained to excel in playing the object of desire and finds that the most effective way to express her independence is to use her performance to shock. She enjoys tantalizing males, but she sometimes shows a disturbed substratum of angry resentment at being taken for granted as a sexual object. In the Children's Games chapter (II.1), Issy speaks collectively with a chorus of seven rainbow girls who protest their condition in a militant tone.

In 1930 Joyce wrote to Weaver of this three-page chorus, "the girl angels sing a hymn of liberation around Shawn" (*SL* 355). The penultimate paragraph of this liberating hymn focuses on a transformation that heralds a concluding assertion of women's independence in political and sexual terms. Before this transformation, the girls are involved in the traditional feminine role, as modeled on the Virgin Mary. They change "sursum corda," or "lift your heart," into the more phallic "lift your tail," saying that when they are tempted, they need a male tube to supplement what their hands could do: "Upsome cauda! Behose our handmades for the lured!" (*FW* 239.9–10). Mary's "Behold the handmaid of the Lord" (Luke 1.38) is an acceptance of servitude, but the girls are about to pass into a new state.

Up to now they have depended on man's armatures and been nuns or mere amateurs, but now they will possess their own openings: "To these nunce we were but yours in ammatures yet well come that day we shall ope to be ores" (*FW* 239.10–12). They will open to reveal riches within by being more "ours" than "yours" ("ores"). Then they will see things clearly and there will be no more pretending, no more giving to men: "No more hoaxites! Nay more gifting in mennage!" *wrong* (*FW* 239.12–13). When they find their own treasure within themselves, there will be no more false gold, or "hoaxites." (German *Hochzeit* means "wedding.") This is an image of heaven, in which there will be no more marriage, and I will return to the idea that woman bears heaven within her body. Admittedly, there is a sarcastic level on which the desires of women for personal freedom are seen in conventional terms as immoral. On this level, as student Rhonda Toussaint pointed out, the girls "hope to be whores." But such cynical undertones do not prevent the elaboration of a new womanly order in the next paragraph:

Hightime is ups be it down into outs according! When there shall be foods for vermin as full as feeds for the fett, eat on earth as there's hot in oven. When every Klitty of a scolderymeid shall hold every yardscullion's right to stimm her uprecht for whimsoever, whether on privates, whather in publics. And when all us romance catholeens shall have ones for all amanseprated. And the world is maidfree. Methanks. So much for his Meignysthy man! And all his bigyttens. So till Coquette to tell Cockotte to teach Connie Curley to touch Cattie Hayre and tip Carminia to tap la Chérie. . . . (*FW* 239.16–25)

The idea of a utopia of "feeds for the fett, eat on earth" reflects the fact that for a long time, and increasingly in this century, women have caused misery for themselves continually by withholding food that they needed or desired, and this was ultimately done to please men. The first level of meaning in this passage, however, as Fritz Senn first pointed out, is a call for suffrage, the main feminist issue of the first quarter of the century. The German for suffrage is *Stimmrecht*, literally, "voiceright," which implies the right to be heard. "Foods for vermin," a misogynist line that shows the tendency of Joyce's mind to breed them, is "votes for women." The right to be heard is linked to sexual freedom here, and the specific nature of this freedom shows Joyce to be more aware of women's desires than previously.

The first sentence says it is high time that women got what is suitable for them. Roland McHugh indicates that this is a parody of Mary's line about the Incarnation, "Be it done unto me according to thy word" (Luke 1.38).[9] Issy and her cohort are asking for "according," which is a courting, but at this point they introduce a specific act that should be done unto women. This is indicated by "down into outs" and confirmed by all the references to eating. It is oral sex, in which one partner goes down into what the other puts out. The implied "according to thy word" also designates orality, and this reading of Luke gives Mary the power to tell how she wants the act done. She gets what she asks for in the sense that the Immaculate Conception traditionally consists of God's putting His Word into her ear.

The chorus proclaims that every woman has a right to have her clitoris stimulated into uprightness whenever she wants. Thus woman will be emancipated or "amanseprated" in that her pleasure no longer depends on his. If sex has to be intercourse, then woman must soothe man's ego so that he can get the necessary erection (and invade her body); but Joyce envisions a shift toward outercourse. This is a fundamental step toward Irigaray's goal of recognizing woman's desire as it might be if it were not dependent on man's.

It is an advance over Molly's situation, for Molly has to wait on a man's sexual pleasure for her own. She says, "I wished he was here or somebody to let myself go with and come again" (U 18.584–85). After her encounter with Blazes, she seems to count her orgasms by counting his, which she first estimates as 3 or 4, then 4 or 5, and then 5 or 6 (U 18.143, 895, 1511). But a woman is capable of having many more orgasms than a man, and Issy's crew takes the position not only that a man should provide them, but that if he can't give them to her, she'll find a woman who can.

So much for his majesty man, with his royal mien, who imposes his mind and pleasure on woman by being his "mine is thy." He can be replaced by a return to the basics, and the classics, of Sapphic education, which teaches girls to touch each other. That these girls can be as active as boys is indicated by the name "Cockotte" and by the image of taking virginity: "to tap la Chérie." Like all sexuality in Joyce, these images are symbolic; in this case, they represent woman's right to be attended to and given pleasure, and they include the right of women to communicate with each other and act collectively. Issy's vision conceives of woman as being separated from man so that "the world is maidfree."

There are many passages in the *Wake* that associate male homosexuality and lesbianism with revolution and utopia respectively. The major gay example is the recurring scene in which Buckley shoots the Russian General (mainly on *FW* 337–55), which serves to make explicit the homosexual and revolutionary undertones in most of the scenes of son-father conflict. We will examine other lesbian-utopian passages.

The limitations of Joyce's radical vision of gender are reflected by a tendency toward salaciousness with Issy, as they are by sentimentality with Anna. The third way in which he always aims at women is by way of seduction. Moreover, showing off how much he knows about women's intimacy is a form of appropriation. In the "Circe" episode of *Ulysses*, Lipoti Virag, the lecherous grandfather moth, says, "All possess bachelor's button discovered by Rualdus Columbus. Tumble her. Columble her" (*U* 15.2341–42). There is a joke here about imperialism, for just as Native Americans discovered America before Columbus, so women must have known about the clitoris before Rualdus Columbus (1519–59), the first anatomist to mention it officially (Gifford and Seidman 493). Historically, the patriarchal order puts women in positions where men discover their sexuality for them: "Columble her." And Joyce's recognition of the repression of women could lead to presumptuousness, as in his statement in the epigraph to my present chapter, from "Ibsen's New Drama" (1900, *CW* 64), that Ibsen knows women better than they know themselves. On the other hand, Joyce was grateful to Nora for having "made me a man" (*Letters I* 233). Since he had been practicing sex with prostitutes, it was not just sex that made him a man, but love. In fact, he maintains that only contact with the feminine can make manhood bearable.

The fact that Issy's chorus speaks to Shaun implies a criticism of their assertions, probably because Joyce saw suffragettes as linked to puritanism, as they sometimes were. They opposed sexual freedom partly because it was generally defined in male terms. Feminists have often criticized Joyce for his persistent emphasis on sexuality, which can disturb women (and men). But one of the points that Issy and company may be making in their rebellious aspect is that women should have a right to full, active sexuality, free from the sanctity of the cloister. Censorship threatens not only Joyce, but many works of feminism, from Sappho (most of whose lyrics are lost) to Jane Campion's film *The Piano*, which could never have been made as it was without the efforts of artists like Joyce. A harder argument to answer is that what is objectionable in Joyce's work is not the amount of sex, but its obsessive nature. My best reply to this is that obsession is what drives Joyce to explore and reveal sexuality in writing.

It is true that Joyce makes women the goal of his works because he wants power over them, and this pattern is examined well by Christine Froula. She argues in "Mothers of Invention" (Friedman 283–303) that because Joyce uses women to express his own fantasies, "it is a mistake to look for female subject positions in Joyce's works" (303). But a woman who portrays a woman will also express her own fantasies. Would a truer female character necessarily be created by a conventional woman writer like Barbara Cartland than by a sympathetically critical man like Joyce or Faulkner? Either the subject position stands for inner depth, in which case any attempt to recreate it would be an approximation that would have to fail in poststructural terms, or it is a political position accessible to reason, so that it should not necessarily be considered out of bounds to a man. Men and women should be able to understand each other, and Joyce contributed to this understanding. Henke's *James Joyce and the Politics of Desire*, the best feminist study of Joyce's works to date, sees Molly as showing the reactions of an actual woman (126–63), and I will build on her recognition of the vitality of Joyce's empathy with the women of the *Wake* (164–212).

Joyce was not the dominating type, and power over women was only part of his motivation in creating them. That another motive may be as important as the desire for power is indicated by the ways in which the women who are the objects of final focus in *Ulysses* and the *Wake* go beyond understanding. Moreover, to a considerable extent they reject their male protagonists, and this is especially true of ALP. There is here a feeling of partaking of the freedom and life force of a woman's mind, and however problematic this freedom may be, it projects valuable possibilities for woman's relationship to man and for her independence.

Yet Joyce's motivation in seeking rejection cannot be encompassed by understanding, addressing, or seducing women. The fourth way he aims at woman is by losing her or alienating himself from her in order to make her and himself sublime. This fourth aspect of love corresponds to the regeneration of the fourth book of the *Wake*, and to the Wakean theme of the fortunate fall (*felix culpa*), in which sin leads to personal development.

Slavoj Žižek (201–31) uses Hegel's and Lacan's ideas to argue that the sublime object can be seen only as negation. Transcendent beauty and absolute knowledge are always represented through paradox, and Žižek holds that the contradiction that reveals the sublime is all we can know of it. The objects that represent the sublime most effectively—such as a skull, money, a sex organ, or a vast perspective—are debased or incomprehensible objects that indicate the impossibility of representing what they stand for.

If the exalted always consists of negation, then the point at which a woman rejects a man is the point at which the transcendent potential of her beauty and vitality appears. Because he cannot escape his male position or compulsion, Joyce can free his women only by having them reject him, or his side. Whether this rejection is permanent must remain suspended in the ambiguity of Joyce's endings. In freeing women to satisfy his own desire for negation, he develops himself in accord with Stephen's intention in *Portrait* to build himself up by sinning, by sundering: "To live, to err, to fall, to triumph, to recreate life out of life!" (*P* 152). Richard Rowan has a similar program in *Exiles*: "To be forever a shameful creature and to build up my soul again out of the ruins of its shame" (*E* 70). These ideas parallel Žižek's (196) observation that the subject constitutes itself by realizing that the sublime object it has believed in is a negation.

Joyce's male protagonists are generally on quests for rejection/ negation, starting with "Araby," in which the hero's epiphany of himself "driven and derided by vanity" is the goal of his quest. Starting with the second page of the *Wake*, HCE is continually engaged in the male project of erecting something that will never stay up for long. The erection he masterbuilds is linked to all of phallocentric civilization and described mockingly as an unstable piling up of syllables: "hierarchitectitiptitoploftical" (*FW* 5.1–2). The fall inherent in it will regenerate him: "Phall if you but will, rise you must" (*FW* 4.15–16).

In *Ulysses*, when Bloom asks Stephen why he left his father's house, Stephen replies, "To seek misfortune" (*U* 16.253), and John Gordon speculates that Bloom may hear this as a reference to a woman named Miss Fortune ("Love" 249). In this case, Bloom's tendency to see a woman behind things may grasp the reality of Stephen's quest. I will return to how the rejection of male authority exalts ALP, but I note here that Joyce frees his heroines because it satisfies his own desire. The pattern of freeing the female by negating the male is active in every substantial unit of Joyce's fiction.

GENDER INTERCHANGE

One reason that Joyce's works focus on the minds of women is that he sees masculinity as a nightmare from which he must flee. Joyce made a remark to his brother Stanislaus that might seem intolerant if it came from a woman: "There are only two forms of love in the world, the love of a mother for her child and the love of a man for lies" (*JJ* 293); and Ellmann remarks that for Joyce, relations between men always have an undertone of hostility (*JJ* 312).

The structural pattern of all of Joyce's major units of fiction is one that develops a masculine conflict that leads to resolution in the mind of a woman. This pattern is reflected in "The Dead" insofar as Gabriel Conroy has to confront the mind of his wife Gretta at the end. In each of the five chapters of *Portrait* Stephen runs into a conflict with a father figure that forces him to wander off to find, at the end of each chapter, a new mother surrogate to release him from the unbearable situation of masculinity.[10] The monologues of Molly and ALP that end *Ulysses* and the *Wake* bring relief from the unresolvable male conflicts that make up most of both works. Joyce expressed a feeling that masculine logic required feminine release at the end of *Ulysses*, that it took "the acidities of Ithaca—a mathematico-astronomico-physico-mechanico-geometrico-chemico sublimation of Bloom and Stephen (devil take 'em both) to prepare for the final amplitudinously curvilinear episode *Penelope*" (*JJ* 501).

Stephen Dedalus' story is framed as a relentless attack on masculine authority. His main theoretical statement, in the "Scylla and Charybdis" episode of *Ulysses*, presents Shakespeare as a man driven to assert a symbolic manhood because he feels he lacks its reality. Manhood is constituted as a reaction against passivity in Joyce, as it is in Lacan. In *Portrait*, when Stephen loses his virginity, he has to be driven to it by a sense of being raped by "some dark presence moving irresistibly upon him. . . . his hands clenched convulsively and his teeth set together as he suffered the agony of its penetration" (*P* 95). His sex drive, which is oppressive in that it aims to use a prostitute, is driven by anxiety about his manhood, anxiety that works as a symbolic father sodomizing him. I don't think that Joyce felt that other men were different, only less conscious, and Lacan, in "The Meaning of the Phallus," says that the phallus is always based on a reaction against a threat (*Feminine Sexuality* 75).[11]

At the start of *Ulysses* Buck Mulligan announces to Stephen, "you have that cursed jesuit strain in you, only it's injected the wrong way" (*U* 1.211). This is an image of the Eucharist as a suppository. It corresponds to Stephen's idea that the relation between father and son is basically one of violent opposition. The establishment is a thorn in his backside. In *Portrait* Stephen identified the Holy Spirit with his personal integrity, but now he sees his identity as a man as a supposition thrust into him, rendering him passive.

Masculine is traditionally associated with active, and feminine with passive, but Freud held that everyone contained both genders. And Lacan argues that since Freud's phallus is a symbol rather than an organ, and since it is always a reaction against passivity, a woman can possess it as readily as a man insofar as society grants her the power to signify. Lacan emphasizes that the genders are constructed by society rather than inherent. He sees masculine and feminine as language systems, both of which are used by everyone (*FS* 47–49).

Ulysses subverts conventional genders by presenting a marriage in which what attracts Bloom most about Molly is her active ability to have an affair, and what draws her most in him is his passive ability to empathize with a woman. The problems that weaken their marriage spring from their inability to recognize these reversals. The novel not only celebrates Bloom as "the new womanly man," but portrays in a searching and insistent way the attraction of dominant women.

Another principle of gender in Joyce is that men and women create each other, a version of Giordano Bruno's idea that everything has to react against its opposite in order to form itself. I will examine Joyce's elaboration of the ways in which women are circumscribed by male systems, and of the ways in which men are shaped by women. The protagonist of the *Wake*—who may be named Humphrey Chimpden Earwicker, and who is represented by the conjunction of any three words beginning with *H*, *C*, and *E*—is presented as written by Anna, who is constituted by *A*, *L*, and *P*: "a huge chain envelope, written in seven divers stages of ink . . . every pothook and pancrook bespaking the wisherwife, superscribed and subpencilled by yours A Laughable Party . . ." (*FW* 66.13–17). The initials are useful because they remind us that the characters take a different form every time they appear. As the letter ALP writes, HCE exists only in transmission from her and to her. A pothook is a kind of writing stroke, and since the seven colors of the rainbow stand for ALP's attractions, she writes him with her desire. That the genders create each other means that neither actually exists outside the circuit in which they are involved. In my fifth chapter, on marriage, I will show how the *Wake* develops the idea that it is artificial to try to isolate genders from the unstable interchange that shapes them. But such emphasis on how the sexes depend on each other causes a problem for feminism because the system of this dependence is organized in a deeply unfair way.

While the idea of improving gender relations by maximizing the interchange of active and passive is a strong one that is built up extensively in *Ulysses* and the *Wake*, a further level of theory is needed to carry women beyond the existing patriarchal structure. Irigaray argues that even if the phallus is undercut, as long as the traditional gender polarity remains in control, woman's sexuality is identified with the clitoris as inferior phallus, and her own pleasure is excluded. Irigaray (23–33) says that woman has pleasure in herself constantly from her two labia touching, so that unlike man, she does not need an instrument or manipulation to give herself enjoyment. While man is obsessed with the phallic climax, woman is open to a variety of pleasures without control.

Patrick McGee applies Irigaray's ideas to Issy effectively: he sees her as using the sliding language of the *Wake* to call for a pleasure outside any fixed form, as pleasure tends to be. McGee allows us to see how Joyce promotes an escape from the active-passive polarity into a feminine free pleasure. This clarifies the theoretical import of the feminine flow that such critics as Scott (*James Joyce*, 95–104, 122–26) and Bishop (336–85) have celebrated in the *Wake*.[12] Moreover, there are indications beyond McGee's that Issy corresponds to Irigaray's idea of feminine pleasure. Joyce used sigla or geometrical signs to represent his figures in the *Wake* as functions. The siglum for Issy is ⊣, but she tends to be accompanied by her mirror-friend Maggy or Madge, who may be either another girl or a reflection, and to whom she continually speaks. As McGee (87–88) points out, it is often hard to tell whether she is speaking to Maggy or to a boy, usually her conventional brother Shaun. The siglum for the total structure of Issy and Maggy combined is ⊣⊢, an image of two lips pressing each other. And Issy's gross language can be explicit about the physical basis of this specular imagery: "Pussy is never alone, as records her chambrette, for she can always look at Biddles and talk petnames with her little playfilly when she is sitting downy on the ploshmat" (*FW* 561.35–562.1).

The problem with seeing Issy as expressing woman's pleasure beyond polarity (and this problem relates to Irigaray's vision) is that Issy is vain, aggressive, and conventional. She is continually linked to phrases like "the law of the jungerl" (FW 268 note 3) and "the so-wiveall of the prettiest" (FW 145.27). The revolutionary passage from Issy and her friends cited earlier shows them asserting phallic power by insisting that every clitoris must be served to make it upright. Issy's tempting discourse easily slips into a dare that dominates. A typical example is one of the footnotes from the Lesson chapter (II.2). These notes add up to one of the main expressions of Issy, and as notes they are both in a subordinate position and in a position of authority. This note refers to a passage about infidelity: "Have you ever thought of a hitching your stern and being ourdeaned, Mester Bootenfly, here's me and Myrtle is twinkling to know" (291 note 4). Issy accepts Shaun, her respectable brother, who pretends piety while enjoying perverse satisfaction under the surface; but she rejects Shem, the sensitive brother who reveals his desires. Here she asks Shaun to marry her and be a repressed but prurient clergyman like Laurence Sterne or Dean Swift. McHugh points out a reference to Emerson's line "Hitch your wagon to a star." But she also asks him to bind up his rear end and take orders (the base meaning of "be ordained"), and it turns out that on one level her friend Myrtle is a switch for flagellation.[13]

There is an 1882 photograph of Paul Ree and Friedrich Nietzsche hitched to a wagon in which the intellectual beauty Lou Salome sits holding a whip (Biddy Martin 74). It is unlikely that Joyce saw this shot, but it may represent a trend. The image of men pulling women in a carriage recurs in III.2, the main scene between Shaun and Issy's troop. The "girls" are described as being in a charabanc, or a chair with a bang: "the cherubs in the charabang, set down here and sedan chair, don't you wish you'd a yoke or a bit in your mouth" (FW 469.34–35). When Issy says, "You want to be slap well slapped for that" (FW 148.6), the emphasis is on "want." Sexual symbols in the Wake represent undercurrents and implications—in this case, the aggressiveness of beauty, the idea of a bello behind every bella, what Stephen calls "woman's invisible weapon" (U 9.461). Irigaray may argue that this weapon is not really woman's, but man's projection.

McGee (91) claims that Issy marries Shaun because this emotional vacuum will allow her to commune with herself, but McGee realizes that the liberating aspect of Issy's discourse does not cover the whole of her personality. He holds that figures in the Wake cannot be covered by any description. Issy's potential for freedom is bound to be enclosed by the patriarchal economy that shapes her womanhood as an object of exchange. This is why her discourse must be deconstructed to see its potential—which is something Joyce's technique does by destabilizing the normative meanings of her words.

But if evaluating Issy poses a problem, there are problems with the views of Irigaray too. She claims that women have access to a sexuality free from active and passive polarities; but it is hard to see how one person can relate to another at all without activity and passivity. In fact, feminist political analysis indicates that when one person looks at or talks to another, the categories of gaze and object, or speaker and listener, bring active and passive into play. Irigaray's support of sexuality without activity seems to privilege autoeroticism over relating to people.

She also claims that in the obscure preoedipal stage girls are already different from boys. This tends toward essentialism, emphasis on inherent qualities, as if the biological difference between the genders entailed two different mentalities. A recent researcher, Irene Fast (10, 13), agrees with Irigaray that Freud was wrong to think of the clitoris as an organ with male feelings; but she holds that the sexual experience of children before the oedipal phase (around five) is "undifferentiated" (4), that "early in development both boys and girls do assume that they have characteristics of both sexes" (12).

A feminist critic of Irigaray, Elizabeth L. Berg, says, "It would seem that any attempt to define woman as rigorously Other than man—to remove her from all possible complicity with the phallologocentric system—ends by situating woman in the place of truth or origin, and thereby describing her in terms of a metaphysics of presence" (18). Seeing this as idealization, Berg prefers a concept of woman as bisexual.

Whether women seek power at the risk of claiming the phallus, or seek to assert their difference from the phallus at the risk of essentialism, the basic problem may be that feminism is not a general theory, but the advocacy of a group. Of course, it may be that no theory can avoid advocacy, and Irigaray (72–85) argues that the mainstream of Western philosophical logic and objectivity has always been a system of abstractions designed to subordinate women. The result of reasonable behavior is summed up by Terry Eagleton's account of women: "there was no time in history at which a good half of the human race had not been banished and subjected as a defective being, an alien inferior" (149). In view of this, it may be necessary to remember the dangers of advocacy while using it to correct a colossal injustice. Women can't be given equality without being given their own minds, and they may need to project ideals (as men always have) in order to build such constructions.

Therefore there is a crucial validity in Irigaray's argument that the traditional polarity is phallocentric and that we need to move toward the unknown area of what woman's feelings would be like if they were not controlled by this system. In accepting the practical necessities of relationship, one accepts cultural constraints that make those necessities seem inevitable, but such constraints may be caused by history. Looking into the excluded sensitivities of women may lead us to subtler modes of relation.

In a critique of Lacan's view of sexuality in his twentieth volume of seminars, *Encore*, Irigaray says, "Psychoanalytic theory thus utters the truth about the status of female sexuality and about the sexual relation. But it stops there. Refusing to interpret the historical determinants of its discourse—" (102). Lacan's truth about the sexual relation is that it does not exist, and from Irigaray's point of view, this is because men use women for male purposes. Thus, she grants that Lacan's ideas recognize what has been going on between the genders, but says he does not see that the existing situation has been produced by historical forces and so may be changed. She says that "if the relation were to come about, everything that has been stated up to now would count as an effect-symptom of its avoidance" (91). I believe she underestimates *Encore*, which, as Jacqueline Rose argues, holds that the existing idea of woman will have to be replaced by something else (see *FS* 48–51, 151–60, and 167–68).

The two views opposed here—that active-passive polarities are needed and that they should be surpassed—correspond to a major schism in feminism described by Toril Moi; many American feminists focus on power for women, but the *écriture féminine* critics, whom Irigaray follows, want to extend feminism outside the structure of power. Sandra M. Gilbert and Susan Gubar (261) attack the *Wake* from the American side in *No Man's Land I*, where they say that Joyce's supposed feminine flow is really masculine compression. Joyce combines both, and anyone who doubts that the *Wake* flows should listen to Joyce's wonderful recording of the end of the ALP chapter, which I recommend as a support for this book. Gilbert and Gubar (232) contradict the idea of male compression when they say that ALP's discourse is the brainless babble of a stereotype. They argue against *écriture féminine* in arguing against Joyce.

The French, influenced by Lacan's idea that any claim to significance is phallic, see the Americans as replacing one chauvinism with another, while the Americans maintain that women who go on focusing on their pure inner feelings will go on being abused by men. This is the difference between realpolitik and idealism. As Moi (13) points out, it is necessary to address political realities, but to avoid "inverted sexism" by remembering the deconstructive position that women have special access to because they have been excluded from power. A similar compromise seems advisable with regard to the two solutions to the gender problem, exchanging genders versus going beyond them: the truth is that both must be used. It is necessary to insist on the need for freedom from polarity, but such freedom may not be obtainable merely by claiming it. Perhaps it is only by balancing the interplay of active and passive between people that we can approach in practice the goal of going beyond polarity. Irigaray seems to see that polarity must be escaped through interchange when she says that in her new conception of language "there would no longer be either a right side or a wrong side of discourse . . . but each passing from one to the other . . ." (80). The alternation of the sides would make the artificiality of the division apparent. Seeing the need to tune in on such interchange, we must understand how gender polarities operate—and that they are very different from the simplified stereotypes of active male and passive female—if we are to enable ourselves to pass beyond them.

Perhaps because women have been withheld from decisive positions, they seem to Joyce to have a special ability to bring about the oscillation needed to break down oppositions through their indifference, their fluidity, their hitherandthithering—three terms Joyce applied to women throughout his career—as opposed to the male compulsion to assert fixity embodied by the tower HCE. The pattern is acted out in the first chapter of the Wake in the tale of Jarl van Hoother and the Prankquean (FW 21–23). The Jarl is isolated in his tower laying cold hands on himself when the Prankquean invades him and forces him to open up. As HCE, the Jarl expresses himself through the polarity of his two sons, Shem the artist and Shaun the conformist. These opposite sons appear here as Tristopher and Hilary. In her campaign against the Jarl, the Prankquean kidnaps Tristopher and converts him into Hilary (FW 21.29–30); then she kidnaps Hilary and converts him into Tristopher (FW 22.16). Rose and O'Hanlon (20n) tell us that the story illustrates Giordano Bruno's motto "In tristitia hilaris hilaritate tristis" (In sadness cheerful, in gaiety sad), a version of the idea that everything contains its opposite. By reversing polarities, the Prankquean breaks down the Jarl's system of distinctions, a forceful version of what a woman does when a man is strongly attracted to her.

The feminine space in which she enacts this reversal, the place she kidnaps the twins to, is referred to at one point as "Woeman's Land" (*FW* 22.8). Based on Grace O'Malley, a bold Irish piratess of the Elizabethan era, the Prankquean is one of the first heroines of the *Wake*.

Such deconstruction of hierarchy is a central activity of ALP and Issy, and they are associated with a series of rebellious heroines in their struggle to liberate themselves from the phallocratic order. Issy represents the hope of youth, but ALP represents the engagement of that hope with reality. Anna, who is what Issy will become, is deeply involved in human relationships, whereas Issy's relations seem phantasmal. These are some reasons why I focus mainly on ALP's presentation as the most fully articulated development of women's position in the *Wake*.

As David Hayman (112) points out, Joyce made a sophisticated statement of Issy's relation to ALP in his 1923 ur-workbook for the *Wake* (Notebook VI.B.3) when he wrote

> Mum-letterwriter
> Is—her libido
> the Beyond (*JJA* 29.241)

As ALP's libido, Issy has to be implicated in the patriarchal order of sexuality, but she also expresses a desire for freedom that reaches beyond existing knowledge of human possibilities.

Both ALP and Issy are hemmed in by the power of traditional, male-oriented authority to shape their minds. In the ALP chapter, the longest section I deal with, this power is represented by two washerwomen, one on either bank of Anna Liffey, who embody the conventional polarities of society that shape the river of ALP's life.

The bondage of women to masculine society is expressed ironically by ALP's frequent appearance as an African. This pattern exposes a widely known equation of the nineteenth century between woman's sexuality and racial inferiority. It also links women to the most terrible injustice and the most urgent need for liberation.

In the concluding chapter of the book, ALP is still entangled in her attachment to her man, but she feels the unfairness of that attachment and yearns for a life of her own. In the end, she rejects HCE and the male order and determines to find her own truth as a woman. Her interaction with this truth may be seen in two different ways, and I present opposing views of the fate of women's liberation in two concluding chapters. ALP's rejection causes her to dread being overwhelmed by a terrifying father figure, but there is a level of her that does not give in.

She is finally in the tragic situation of Antigone, as analyzed by Lacan: her rejection of the Symbolic order leads her outside of life and makes her enact the crime involved in woman's feelings. Lacan describes the point of rebellion Antigone reaches as the source of renewal for civilization, and ALP's turning away is the ultimate goal of the *Wake*, the negation that motivates the whole book.

As her last word, "the," leads into the *Wake*'s first one, "riverrun," she takes on the entire narrative in reaching the chapel of her lost womanhood. This chapel is identified with the Egyptian sky goddess Nut, and at the end, while ALP is frightened by a vision of father ocean, she foresees herself leaving the ocean behind as she evaporates to return to her mother in the sky. Her return to her Egyptian mother links her womanly nature as primal source to the potential of the non-Western world, the unknown from which the future will come.

2

Two Songs

THE SONG OF DEBORAH

To indicate some structural principles of the *Wake*, I will examine the organizational complexity of a pair of motifs that are connected to the idea of the waking of women into liberation. This theme is part of the fundamental level of the *Wake* on which the lives we live are dreams from which we might wake. Joyce was explicit about this idea in discussing Arnold Rubek, the protagonist of Ibsen's *When We Dead Awaken*, when he reviewed that play in 1900: "Thus in the conversion of Rubek's views as to the girl-figure in his masterpiece, 'The Resurrection Day,' there is involved an all-embracing philosophy, a deep sympathy with the cross-purposes and contradictions of life, as they may be reconcilable with a hopeful awakening—when the manifold travail of our poor humanity may have a glorious issue" (CW 66). I grant that Joyce increasingly enclosed such hopes in irony, so that they could be seen only as possibility rather than actuality. Ultimately, they might be only mirage, but such a possibility remained part of his vision.

In this passage it is the conversion that involves the all-embracing philosophy. It is change that gives sympathy with the cross-purposes and contradictions of life, and it is this shifting, a feminine feature generated by Rubek's vision of a "girl-figure," that will lead to the awakening of humanity. So humanity will awake through the feminine, which will reconcile the contradictions of life by embracing shift, by replacing, in Irigaray's terms, the logic of either/or with that of both/and (Grosz 176). The *Wake* aims at such awakening through both its construction and its texture.

At the age of sixteen Joyce impressed his French teacher by invoking "the term *idée-mère* as the French equivalent for leitmotif" (*JJ* 60). The

French phrase "mother idea" usually means the basic idea of a literary work. I call the motifs or scattered repeating phrases that I examine songs because they are made of music, as motifs originally were and as virtually all of the *Wake* is.

An earlier generation of *Wake* critics, led by Clive Hart, mapped out many of the major motifs of the *Wake* with the aim of putting them together into coherent structures. Recent critics have often been more concerned with pointing out incoherencies than with putting things together. The shift in emphasis, which was influenced by poststructuralism, has generally been a shift away from masculine, phallocentric values to feminine values of dissemination.

The deconstructive function of the *Wake*, its taking apart of meanings, is one of its strongest aspects. While it should not be taken to preclude specific interpretations of the text, it serves to indicate that they depend on different perspectives and are displaceable. I am aiming here at finding relatively coherent feminist meanings in the *Wake*, but hope to avoid the kind of closure that patriarchy is built on; so I find it appropriate that the material I examine embodies the status of women by being displaced from integration. The two songs I focus on are barely there, are distributed in an incoherent way that makes them represent a suppressed and decentered level of the text. They are marginal, as women are often assumed to be.

Joyce's women, however, make an impression. And at one point in the tale of Jarl van Hoother and the Prankquean, the Prankquean converts Hilary by making an impression on him: "she punched the curses of cromcruwell with the nail of a top into the jiminy . . ." (*FW* 22.14–15). Grace Eckley (*Children's Lore* 109–10) points out that the image of a woman putting a nail into a man's head refers to the Israelite Jael, who hammers a nail into the temple of the Canaanite leader Sisera in the Song of Deborah, the fifth chapter of Judges (verse 26).

The Song of Deborah, generally regarded as one of the best poems in the Bible, was written around 1100 B.C. by a woman. Commentators have almost always denied female authorship for Judges 5, saying that the opening words, "Then sang Deborah and Barak . . ." are only conventional, and the repeated use of the pronoun that the King James version (which Joyce seems to echo) translates as "I" is ambiguous (James Martin 62, 64). Only recently have feminists such as Mieke Bal (209–10) and Lois Galbraith Dickie (35–70) given Deborah credit as an author.

Joyce apparently believed Deborah to be the authoress of the Song. He was attracted to Samuel Butler's *The Authoress of the Odyssey*. Joyce's taste for debatable theories may have been related to his position as an Irishman who recognized a suppressed aspect of history that could be recovered only by speculation. Moreover, Joyce seems to entertain the controversial theory that matriarchy preceded patriarchy in the ancient world. This is indicated in one version of a passage from Edgar Quinet that gets repeated a lot in the *Wake* (Hart 182–200). The passage says that flowers have kept dancing across the centuries while mighty empires have come and gone, so it favors feminine values over masculine ones.

The last version of this motif, which precedes ALP's final letter, says, "since the days of Plooney and Columcellas, when Giacinta, Pervenche and Margaret swayed over the all-too-ghoulish and illyrical and innumantic in our mutter nation" (*FW* 615.2–4). McHugh notes that Pliny and Columella were Romans who wrote about nature, while *giacinto* is Italian for hyacinth, and *pervenche* and *marguerite* are French for periwinkle and daisy. Finally, Gaul, Illyria, and Numantia were ancient realms. Since the three flowers have women's names, we can conclude that in the distant past women held sway over mother nations. *Mutter* is German for "mother," but the passage also implies that since then, the mother nation has become a "mutter nation," a society delineated by things women have said under their breaths. This is what Showalter (201) refers to as "the 'wild zone' of woman's culture" outside male rational articulation. Joyce describes this nation as all-too-girlish, lyrical, and mathematically illiterate (innumerate).

Such matriarchy, which may be prehistoric because male history has suppressed it, corresponds to Harold Bloom's theory in *The Book of J.* He argues that the earliest and most fundamental parts of Genesis were written by a woman, but they were later covered over by layers of male writing (Bloom and Rosenberg 15). Bloom's speculation may help us to see a woman's point of view strongly expressed in the fourth and fifth chapters of Judges, the seventh book of the Bible.[1]

Chapter 4 says that Deborah is a judge and prophet of Israel to whom the people come for guidance (4.4–5). When the Canaanites under Sisera rise to oppress (or resist) the Israelites, Deborah decides there should be a battle and calls on Barak to lead the host. But Barak is afraid to go without her: "And Barak said unto her, if thou wilt go with me, then I will go; but if thou wilt not go with me *then* I will not go" (4.8). Under Deborah's leadership, the Israelites win, and she sings her song with her subordinate Barak. She celebrates the murder of Sisera by the terrorist Jael and compares the victorious Hebrew army to a river overflowing and sweeping away the Canaanites (5.21).

The *Wake* refers to ALP as "diva deborah" in part III, chapter 1, where she is seen (apparently) leading a group of women in a circle around HCE who are compared to biblical dancers (*FW* 415.4). The word *diva*, which is applied to Anna repeatedly (*FW* 492.8, 560.2), combines "singer" with "goddess," and is now enjoying a certain vogue partly because it represents the most commanding kind of woman. Joyce here recognizes the authority of Deborah in connection with ALP.

In an earlier section (II.3), HCE is so massive and lethargic that he is described as looking exactly like a god, "Deblinity devined" (*FW* 373.20). This image of male grossness as the city of Dublin seems so far in meaning from "diva deborah" that they have little in common but sound. And this pattern, which corresponds to the wildly differing versions of ALP and HCE, carries the implication that all continuities of meaning are dependent on coincidence. For all languages are built on arbitrary similarities on the material level of the signifier. Yet these two versions of the motif share the power of Deborah as a leader who inspires her people from an unlikely position. Of course, Deborah was a bloodthirsty imperialist, out to conquer Palestine, just as Jael was a terrorist in that she pretended to be friendly to Sisera. But such terms depend on one's viewpoint, and within the biblical tradition, Deborah is a liberator of her oppressed people.

The death of Sisera after Jael nails him gives a good idea why the Song of Deborah is so distinguished, for this verse (5.27), which is followed immediately by a jump cut to a long scene of Sisera's mother waiting for him to return, is perhaps the first slow-motion violence shot in literature: "At her feet he bowed, he fell, he lay down: at her feet he bowed, he fell: where he bowed, there he fell down dead." This appears weirdly transformed at the end of the Children's Games chapter (II.1), as McHugh points out, when the children hear their father coming and run away: "Of their fear they broke, they ate wind, they fled; where they ate there they fled; of their fear they fled, they broke away" (*FW* 258.5–7). Here the main connection to the biblical original is rhythm, and the rhythm lends intensity to the dissolution of childish imagination by adult brutality. What triggers their flight is the sound of HCE farting (*FW* 258.4), which recurs as an ambivalent image of paternal forcefulness.

The rhythm that carries the reference to Deborah here as an undercurrent exemplifies Kristeva's semiotic, the level of maternal pulsation in language (*Revolution* 25–30). What is being vanquished here, as we head for the Study chapter and move from play to work, is a level of sensitivity that corresponds to the poetic side of Deborah, the side that sympathizes with Sisera's mother for some fourteen lines. As the *Wake* puts it, "The timid hearts of words all exeomnosunt" (*FW* 258.2). The Latin refers primarily to *exeunt omnes*, "they all leave." Although it does not appear directly here, Deborah's description of Sisera dying returns at the end of the *Wake* in Anna's "I sink I'd die down over his feet . . ." (*FW* 628.10–11). This shows how something that is not mentioned can enter the economy of the *Wake* by being attached to something that is; for the latter line could not refer to Deborah without the former, yet the former is only a description of children running. The pattern expresses the Wakean idea of nothing being left out.

Since Deborah means "bee," there may be other references to her among the ten references to bees in the *Wake*, virtually all of them female. After making love to HCE in book III, ALP is referred to as a "queenbee" (*FW* 590.28). An especially likely reference to Deborah is "bible bee" (*FW* 256.18), which is close to the passage about children just cited, and is a variation on both bumble and spelling bees. This gets expanded so as to refer to Deborah's renown as a liberator: "Godeown moseys and skeep thy beeble bee" (*FW* 313.5, "Go down, Moses, and set thy people free"). Here again we can see how dense the network of connections is that courses with submerged meanings.

Deborah, then, is a continuing presence (though never a full one) in the *Wake*, and wherever she is referred to she tends to represent the main theme of her song: "Awake, awake, Deborah: awake, awake, utter a song: arise, Barak, and lead thy captivity captive . . ." (Judges 5.12). This non-Western invocation may be called one of the first revolutionary passages in Western literature because what Deborah determines to imprison is captivity itself: she defines herself as fighting and singing not for or against any person, but for freedom against oppression.

Variations of this line seem to carry on its progressive impact. Saint Paul clarifies the principle by leaving out the pronoun when he says that Christ "led captivity captive" (Ephesians 4.8). Shelley gives it more life when he proclaims the liberation of humanity in *Prometheus Unbound*: "And Conquest is dragged Captive through the Deep" (line 556). In the *Wake*, as I will show, this line takes a new turn to become an antirape slogan that passes through ALP's field of consciousness. The power of Deborah's words to carry so far has to do with their aiming forward into history. This is the song of a militant woman calling on herself to awake and calling on a man to follow her, calling them to join in a joyful struggle to free humanity from oppression; and it is woven

into the story of Anna, her husband, and her daughter. The song of
Deborah is the song of Dawn.

THE SONG OF DAWN

A heliotrope envelope was lying beside his breakfast-cup and he was caressing
it with his hand. Birds were twittering in the ivy and the sunny web of the
curtain was shimmering along the floor: he could not eat for happiness.
—"The Dead"

The singing of women is associated in the *Wake* with another motif, the
singing of birds in the woods. The longest passage to develop this image occurs in the Tavern scene (II.3), when HCE's customers ask for a
song: "What we warn to hear, jeff, is the woods of chirpsies cries to
singaloo sweecheeriode and sock him up, the oldcant rogue" (*FW*
359.18–20). The last six words show that what they want is an attack on
the patriarch HCE. The rebellious nature of this attack may be under-
lined by the allusion to the Afro-American spiritual "Swing Low,
Sweet Chariot." While what the customers get may be revolutionary, it
is neither the spiritual nor the English roustabout song "Knocked 'em
in the Old Kent Road": it is the "dewfolded song of the naughtingels"
(*FW* 359.32).[2] This cheery ode, which goes on for over two pages, is
evidently a radio broadcast, and as Rose and O'Hanlon (189) point out,
it consists of Issy and her mirror image singing to each other. The two-
fold song is equated with all music by a series of about a dozen puns
on composer's names (*FW* 360.7–13). It is identified as the object of desire, what the customers want to hear, a song of naughty girls that
originates from erogenous zones in being "dewfolded."

The feminine object of desire always consists of two girls commun-
ing with each other, corresponding to Irigaray's two lips kissing. A
woman who poses erotically is doubled because she is enjoying *herself*.
At one point in the *Wake* a version of Issy strips "teasily," and when
she exposes her legs, she finds that "her jambs were jimpjoyed to see
each other" (*FW* 68.2). Joyce gets very close to her here as she jumps
for joy, showing his erotic desire to be inside her feelings. He plays the
role of Rualdus Columbus by discovering the feeling of women, who
might not realize how they were doubled by eroticism until he revealed it.

The idea of woodbirdsong as the object of desire is expressed by
Shaun, whose materialism renders it as a song of aristocratic wealth,
when he sees himself "in the birds' lodging, me pheasants among,

where I'll dreamt that I'll dwealth mid warblers' walls when throstles and choughs to my sigh hiehied . . ." (FW 449.17–19). Tim Martin pointed out at a group reading that the last word is sung as an extension of "sigh." As McHugh notes, this is a version of "I Dreamt I Dwelt," which is sung by Maria in "Clay" and was originally sung by Arlene in Michael Balfe's "The Bohemian Girl": "*I dreamt that I dwelt in marble halls / With vassals and serfs at my side*" (D 106). Shaun is dreaming of being in the vibrant womb, "mid warblers' walls." In this place where the walls consist of vibrations of song, there is no separation between internal and external, as is shown by the fact that the birds hie to his sighs, sing to his wishes. He dreams he is the song of the birds.

Lacan says that some men can partake of woman's *jouissance*, or sexual pleasure (FS 147), and this passage suggests that even Shaun can share women's sensitivity. He is guilty of appropriation, but he has feminine feelings in his mind, for the dreams, the sighs, and the warbling song are feminine. Virtually all men have and need strong feminine feelings, but they are trained to repress them, while women are trained to repress their masculine principles.

Shaun's lines echo the ALP chapter, where one of the washerwomen says that the other was crippled by soldiers "when Collars and Cuffs was heir to the town" (FW 214.29), which refers to a period of licentiousness. "Collars and Cuffs," as Glasheen (5) indicates, was the nickname of Albert Victor, duke of Clarence, who lived in Dublin for a time. The Dubliners may have been elated that the toast of their town was heir to the throne, though Albert died before he could become king. Albert lived in the nineteenth century, and the washer was injured, presumably through sexual abuse, early in her life.

In the minds of Waking women the image of birdsong tends to be associated with morning. Issy makes this link in one of her footnotes in the Study chapter. The text, which generally speaks for her parents, says, "For (hushmagandy!) long 'tis till gets bright that all cocks waken and birds Diana with dawnsong hail" (FW 276.17–19). Issy's sixth note reads, "Pipette. I can almost feed their sweetness at my lisplips." McHugh points out that Robert Burns uses "hochmagundy" to mean "copulation." Joyce was familiar with Blake's idea that sexual pleasure leads to a higher level of existence, which is linked to another Blakean idea that is fundamental to the *Wake*, that the ordinary world is a state of sleep from which we will wake through vision, revolution, or sex into a state in which all restraints will disappear. We taste this state at moments of inspiration, and a common form it takes for many people is a light-headed feeling one gets when one wakes in the morning to hear the singing of birds, which begins with dawn. I can remember at such times having a feeling that I was capable of everything (a feeling that wore off as I woke up fully and remembered my problems), and one gets a similar feeling in a state of sexual excitation, all atwitter.

A line that links birdsong to dawn occurs during the radio broadcast in the Tavern scene at a point when marriage is anticipated: "before Sing Mattins in the Fields" (FW 328.24–25). Matins, the first of the canonical hours, stands for morning prayers, and the OED says that Spenser and other poets speak of birds singing matins because they sing in the morning. This line also refers to the martin, a small swallow, and to a church in London, St. Martin's in the Fields, which has been associated with music for centuries.

The passage about Diana in the Study chapter implies that for women in the Wake, the dawn will be the release of their own feelings, suggested here by a breakdown of syntax: "long 'tis till gets bright that all cocks waken." Later we get the jazzy apocalyptic image of a "bugle dianablowing, wild as wild" (FW 475.36–76.1). Diana was a major Mediterranean fertility goddess even though she was a virgin. She preceded classical mythology, and because she was regarded as a "ruler of everything," she is a central figure in feminist efforts to revive powerful goddesses. Her main temple was at Ephesus in Turkey, and she was associated with bees (Goldberg). The temple appears in the Study chapter in a list of the Seven Wonders of the Ancient World (FW 261.11). She is portrayed in Greek mythology as Artemis, a fierce huntress who destroyed men. This leads Joyce to see two girls in the park who occasion HCE's sin as dominant, horsy women: "a deuce of dianas ridy for the hunt" (FW 43.11). Diana is often described as hermaphroditic, and she had for a time a lesbian companion named Kallisto (Kerenyi 146).

Issy's note enters when we are told that the birds hail with dawnsong this guardian of female sanctity. She addresses "Pipette," French argot for pipe (McHugh), and a reference to the little pipes of birdsong. Pipette is a variant of a nickname she uses so that it is often hard to tell whether she is addressing a boy or her girl pal Maggy, but it usually refers to her incestuous boyfriend Shaun.

Her note is a parody of Gerty Macdowell, who can "almost feel" Bloom's lips as she watches him staring at her and masturbating yards away (U 13.707). But instead of feeling, Issy feeds, because the awaking she anticipates is generated by her own discourse, particularly by her lipslips. Lipslips are the substance of kissing (together with slips of the tongue), but they are also the sliding of language that constitutes the Other of feminine feeling. Issy is after all talking primarily to her mirror image, looking into herself to find the reality of woman's desire, a reality that is presented here as having the potential to transform the world. Her quest is parallel to that of Stephen Dedalus, who set out to forge in the smithy of his soul the uncreated consciousness of the human race. In fact, there was a passage in "Proteus" where Stephen felt that his lips were kissing other worlds (U 3.401–3).

The visionary implications of this image remain in force when it becomes central to the end of the *Wake*. ALP then says to HCE, "We will take our walk before in the timpul they ring the earthly bells. . . . Or the birds start their treestirm shindy" (*FW* 621.33–36). The reference to *Tristram Shandy* suggests going back to infancy because the hero of that deconstruction spends most of the book being born. The walk on which Anna wants to take HCE will carry him toward the vibration of birdsong that represents release from the alienation of their moribund conventional relationship. Though men want birdsong, it is women who sing it, and it can lead them to the pulsating oscillation of a new consciousness free of opposition.

Singing in itself represents the optimistic aspirations of Issy. In the Study chapter, the line "Singalingalying. Storiella as she is syung" (*FW* 267.7–8) is followed by this line in the left margin: "There was a sweet hopeful called Cis." McHugh tells us that in German "Cis" means "C sharp." This note has a sound that could be called uplifting in a discordant way. But "Singalingalying" includes "lying," and the marginalium has its ironic undertone. This vision of girlhood is bound to be corrupted, and it is in Anna that we see the actual life of women. Yet at the end Anna says she was "lilting on all the time" (*FW* 627.21), meaning she dealt with her troubles by singing. Throughout her life she carried closely the utopian component represented by Issy, the song of dawn.

3

The Voice of the River

GOSSIPACEOUS ANNA

The "Shem" chapter (I.7), which precedes "Anna Livia Plurabelle," ends with Shem as Mercius emotionally announcing at length that "gossipaceous Anna Livia" (195.4) "is acoming" (194.22), a phrase that suggests she consists of joy or *jouissance*. ALP, however, does not seem to appear directly in the chapter that follows, or to speak fully until her letter and soliloquy at the end of the *Wake*. Yet this chapter is her main treatment in the heart of the book, so we must consider how she does appear: as an opposition, a breakdown of the system of co-herencies through which the chapter's discourse is expressed. A likely patois for a river.

The ostensible speakers in this chapter are two washerwomen on either bank of the river whose names are not given until Anna gives them at the end: "Queer Mrs Quickenough and odd Miss Dodd-pebble" (*FW* 620.19). In her essay with this title, Eckley shows that Doddpebble is the one who is always asking to hear of Anna, starting with the opening of the chapter:

> O
> tell me all about
> Anna Livia! I want to hear all
> about Anna Livia. Well you know Anna Livia?
> (*FW* 196.1–4)

Quickenough, who speaks the last sentence, answers Doddpebble by describing ALP and her story. The expansion of the first four lines corresponds to the fact that the river grows steadily wider. By line 4 we are inside it as it reaches the margins, but it continues to grow (implying that a wider page would give longer lines, though there are exceptions), and the washers have more and more difficulty hearing each other as their banks get farther apart.

The breakdown of their rational discourse is the growth of ALP. She is represented and contained by the gossip of the washers, which both opposes and constitutes her. The old women at the end of part I, like the four old men who watch HCE and ALP as Tristan and Isolde at the end of part II, show how gender mentality has to be seen through the archaic voices of tradition: when we act as men or women, we enact ancient concepts built into culture.

John Gordon, who emphasizes the level on which the *Wake* involves a realistic family, says that the washers are the voices of Kate the servant talking to herself (*Plot* 164–65). As an aging member of the proletariat, she combines qualities shown by both washers, being both conservative and radical, both humorous and bitter. Perhaps the river of womanhood that runs through her washes away the stains of the world.

The first page of I.8 concentrates on how grimy HCE's shirt is: "I know by heart the places he likes to saale, duddurty devil! (*FW* 196.14–15). The Saale is one of over eight hundred river names in this chapter, and combines *sail* and *soil* with a bit of brogue. *Sail* and *soil* go together for the embittered washers because, as they see it, a man gets an agreeable sense of floating along when he does something dirty that a woman has to attend to.

A criticism that women frequently level at men is that they seem to think of nothing but sex. Joyce's own mind could hardly be taken to disprove this claim, but he does recognize its validity. For example, when ALP's letter appears near the end, it is addressed to a version of the phrase *dear dirty Dublin*: "Dear. And we go on to Dirtdump" (*FW* 615.12). The assumption that men generally think about sex, while women are not supposed to, constitutes an enactment of a biased system that allows men mentally to push their attention onto women at all times, or to be perpetually impending.

Central to woman's job is knowing exactly where her man likes to do his dirt, so she can mirror his desire to support his phallic identity. His desire may be seen as a perversion that weakens his manhood, like foot fetishism; but if she accepts this desire, it strengthens his manhood. This is a basic level of the image of the women as washers, cleansing man's intimate things.

Margot Norris shows that the washers give full expression to the activities and concerns of working women (*Web* 153–59). There is a joke about not drying clothes efficiently in "Wring out the clothes! Wring in the dew!" (*FW* 213.19–20); but the familiar reference to Tennyson's *In Memorium* ("Ring out the old, ring in the new") indicates that they renew the material of civilization. Thus they are parallel to the vicociclometer, a machine for recycling and transmitting history that appears at the end (*FW* 614.27–615.11) just before ALP's letter.

The working women seem to be the force of production, and Fredric Jameson (89) tells us that the force of production dictates the shape of history. Joyce's version of this force emphasizes the likelihood that most productive work throughout history has been unrecognized work done by women. As Nancy Chodorow (5, 65, 184) points out, in a wide range of societies women are trained from childhood to be useful and to help people, to be "relational," while boys are trained to be independent and to assert themselves in ways that may be destructive. This distinction is built into the *Wake*, and is reflected in the cooperation between the washers that Norris demonstrates. Moreover, their cooperation generates not only productive work, but cultural production as a shaping of life. Joyce's version of such production insists on the power of popular culture in an ironic way, for if thought is shaped by desire, historical narrative may be driven by its idlest level.

The main activity articulated by the discourse of the washers is gossip, which is later equated by Anna with their job of handling dirt: "And when them two has had a good few there isn't much more dirty clothes to publish" (*FW* 620.20). The word *gossip* is traced by Skeat back to the Middle English *gossib*, related in God. It came to mean a sponsor in baptism or a crone. ALP tells us that these crones baptized her sons (*FW* 620.18), and it seems that Quickenough baptized Shem, who is linked to the life principle and the stem, which is why she turns into a tree, while Doddpebble baptized Shaun, so she turns into a stone.

The fact that *gossip* meant "old woman" before it meant "speak of personal life or scandal" indicates an equation between the person and what she is assumed to say. Likewise, the discourse of the gossips constitutes Anna by embodying the conditions to which she is subject, just as the washers stand for the two banks that shape ALP, of whom it is said that "stout stays, the rivals, lined her length" (*FW* 208.14), making them fit her as tightly as a corset.

One of these conditions is the subjection of women to a frustrated, hysterical desire organized by phallic economy. Doddpebble, whose passivity is suggested by her having "won" her "limp" from "husky hussars" in her youth (*FW* 214.28), simply cannot wait to hear more from Quickenough: "Tell me all. Tell me now. You'll die when you hear" (*FW* 196.4–5). The first sentence suggests that Doddpebble will herself be recounted by the narrative. The last, spoken by Quick-enough, is a piece of hyperbole that is literally true, as Eckley points out ("Queer Mrs Quickenough" 204), for the women turn to tree and stone when Anna's story is told and the flow of desire is used up. That the women express the organization of desire that ALP is partly enclosed by is indicated by correspondences between their frame and the story they tell of how Anna was imposed on. At one point Doddpebble says, "Onon! Onon! tell me more. Tell me every tiny teign. I want to know every singul ingul" (*FW* 201.22). McHugh mentions that the Danish *tegn* means "sign" and that the Teign is a river.

"Onon" refers to the nymph Oenone, a figure of woman's uncontrollable desire who illustrates how that desire gets frustrated because it is the man who gets to do the choosing. She was living with Paris when he was called to the judgment that led him to Helen. Oenone spent the rest of her life lamenting, and decades later, when Paris was brought to her mortally wounded, she refused to cure him. Then she changed her mind and rushed to help him, but found him dead, and hung herself. Tennyson's "Oenone," the most famous English version, focuses mainly on the nymph helplessly watching her man being impressed by the beauty of the goddesses.

In lines like "Tell me every tiny teign" the washers speak rivers, generating Anna to illustrate how social forces generate personal feelings. The impetuosity of the desire for gossip may be what constitutes her, so that "go on" changes not only into the name of a river, "Garonne, garonne!" (*FW* 205.15), but also into "go an!" (*FW* 204.27). The gossip itself is the river, for it is made up of flowing liquid: "Drop me the sound. . . . drip me why. . . . trickle me through was she . . ." (*FW* 204.21–23). Like a river, the force of the storytelling that is Anna's substance, the "substrance of a streamsbecoming" (*FW* 597.7–8), cannot be held back: "Where did I stop? Never stop! Continuarration!" (*FW* 205.13–14). Desire is shaped and pressed by social forces, but because it is unstoppable, it alters them and goes beyond them, so it is a force for change.

The story of Oenone as female victim has much in common with gossip, which can reinforce convention and denigrate women. Gossips show their retrograde side in the *Wake* by blaming women for men's faults. As the washers tell the story of ALP and HCE, for example, her sins are described at length (*FW* 202–4), and he is described as being disgraced as a result (*FW* 205). In chapter 4, the public reactions to HCE's disgrace are divided by gender under two rubrics: "Assembly men murmured. Reynard is slow!" (*FW* 97.28) and "Dispersal women wondered. Was she fast?" (*FW* 101.1). Here the men blame him and the women blame her.

On the other hand, gossip, as a women's genre, is able to see the position of women critically. As Aïda Yared pointed out to me, the washers (Quickenough in particular) seem to recognize Oenone's folly: "was Parish worth thette mess" (*FW* 199.8).[1] There is even a revolutionary potential in gossip, for it tends to insist that the rich are at least as bad as the poor, and it faces truths that would not otherwise be revealed, such as the truth of women's victimization seen in Oenone. The washers say of HCE's first getting together with ALP, "He raped her home" (*FW* 197.21). The mild reading of this line is "he brought her home," which is what the early versions said (*JJA* 48.82, 136). But a stronger reading is that he raped her sexually and violated her deep in her soul ("home"), a common experience of wives throughout history. The political effect of gossip depends on how it is used, and the *Wake* goes far toward using gossip to overthrow conventions and to reveal underlying truth, as in this subversive reading of romantic elopement.

Perhaps the most compromising thing that the washers can say about ALP is that she acted as "proxenete" (*FW* 198.17) for her mate: "she was calling . . . sals from all around . . . to go in till him, her erring cheef" (*FW* 198.10–12). A proxenete is a person who negotiates on another one's behalf. It not only means that ALP is a procuress, but suggests that as the object of desire she is approximate or a proxy, and this is shown by HCE's infidelity. For Lacan, the object of desire is always a substitute for something that can never be attained, a pattern that accords with Freud's idea that the ultimate object is the lost mother of infancy.

The washers go on to say that ALP stood in the doorway and signaled passing women, then instructed them on how to excite HCE, throwing any wench at him "no matter what sex" and "two adda tammer" (two at a time, *FW* 200.31). If ALP is meant to be typical here, Joyce seems to be defaming women, but then Lacan says that to be called a woman in the existing language is to be defamed. He plays on the French for "called woman," *dit-femme* (*FS* 156). But all of this has to do with the nature of gossip.

Gossip is one of the folk genres that Bakhtin (23) describes as drawing their object "into the zone of crude contact" where it can be fingered on all sides, exposed, and taken apart. But it may be the only form in some situations to focus on certain important realities. It is a staple of gossip that the most fortunate women in the world—women like Jackie Kennedy and Princess Diana—are afflicted with adulterous husbands. Figures on how many men are unfaithful vary, but at least until recently, infidelity may have been the rule rather than the exception—a rule omitted from polite discourse.[2]

Moreover, because men have usually been in charge, they have generally arrogated for themselves the right to have more than one woman, though there is plenty of evidence that women are capable of desiring the fulfillment of having more than one man. In Eugene O'Neill's *Strange Interlude*, for example, the protagonist, Nina Leeds, has three men, each of whom serves a different purpose for her. Robert Storey (431) cites the anthropologist George Peter Murdock, who concludes that 83 percent of the world's societies have been polygynous, with one man having two or more women. How completely we have been indoctrinated with the ideology of male dominance is indicated by the fact that many anthropologists believe that men are genetically predisposed to have more than one mate.

If, in a supposedly monogamous context, a woman's husband cheats on her, this may well become the main issue of her life; and if she doesn't want to lose him, she has to arrange her life so as to allow him to see the other woman and to keep the secret from family, from society, and perhaps most of all from herself. This may take a lot of daily doing, including putting up with stress; so the situation of such a woman would be in effect the same as Anna's in arranging her husband's adultery. Even if only a minority of women are in this position, it casts a shadow over others, who may be compromised by trying to avoid it. This is one way in which the gossip about Anna recognizes the truth about women.

Another aspect of Anna's arrangements is that one of the main duties of a bourgeois wife was hiring servants, and she might often have to hire them knowing (or denying) that her husband was likely to have ideas about them. In the "Eumaeus" episode of *Ulysses*, Bloom reflects that men "were always hanging around on the waiting list about a lady, even supposing she was the best wife in the world" (*U* 16.1544–46). Since the tendency to notice alternatives would be at least as true for the husband, it leads to the implication that one either restricts one's mate or grants the freedom to connect to some extent with others. This question is emphasized in *Exiles*, where Richard allows Bertha to commit adultery, and in *Ulysses*. To give such freedom is for Joyce a central expression of love, and to withhold it is to deny love.

The traditional double standard asks women to give such freedom and men to withhold it and keep their wives chaste. Moreover, woman is supposed to accept her position, to feel natural in a role that allows man to take advantage of her. If she lacks the devotion that traps her in this position, she is defined as unnatural.

The inconstancy of Joyce's women is caused by their having to live lies. In fact, Joyce presents ALP's violation by male authority as dividing her: when she is seduced, her stream becomes diverted, so that she is forked. This is indicated by a version of Dryden's line from "Alexander's Feast," "None but the brave deserves the fair," identified by McHugh in a line considering where ALP may have been seduced: "where the Braye divarts the Farer" (FW 203.10–11). It is also suggested by "Bifur" (FW 215.19), which suggests *bifurcate*. The opposite of being divided by caring is unifying two streams by "Letting on she didn't care" (FW 198.16). At the end Anna says she often had to recuperate by bringing the channels of her divided feelings together: "And me letting on to meself always" (FW 627.20–21). By bringing her streams together, she recovers the full polyvocal song of woman's discourse before it was divided by men.

The question of where Anna was first divided is pursued avidly by the washers under a rubric based on Coleridge's lines from the "Ancient Mariner," "We were the first that ever burst / Into that silent sea." The washers ask, "Waiwhou was the first thurever burst?" (FW 202.12–13). Woman is supposed to be pure to protect man's sense of manhood as possession—and partly, as Joyce sees, to protect man from homosexual feelings he may have toward other men who have had her. This ideal is another way of putting women in an impossible position, for there is always someone who made an earlier impression on any woman.

Hélène Cixous presents an elaborate analysis of Joyce's belief that a man always finds that the woman he loves has already given her primary allegiance to a previous lover of some sort, and Cixous says that the prior man stands for the father or God (*Exile* 484–503). In this case, the main prior figure is a hermit named Michael Arklow (FW 203.18). He is pious and seems to be linked to the "Father Michael" mentioned in the first version of ALP's letter (FW 111.15). This competitor goes back to Michael Furey in "The Dead" and Father Moran, whom Stephen saw Emma Clery as flirting with in *Portrait* (P 176, 187, 191–92). The main feature that makes this prior figure unbeatable may be his chastity, which casts a spell over the woman: her desire for him is endless because it can never be fulfilled, a pattern established by the father.

Michael plunges his hands in ALP's hair and kisses her forehead with great feeling (*FW* 203.22–204.1). Although he is tempted "to the vierge violetian" (*FW* 203.28–29), or to the verge of violating the virgin, he does not seem to do more. Michael is one of the main names of Shaun, the hypocritical brother. One point of the scene with Arklow is that a woman could remember (consciously or not) a father figure's hands on her hair and his kiss, and try to reproduce them with every lover. Indeed the kiss that Stephen's mother gives him at the beginning of *Portrait* (*P* 21) echoes through his mind and leads to the kisses in the last lines of *Ulysses* and the *Wake*. Irigaray (87) says that in the Freudian construction that woman has generally lived by, she "remains forever fixated on the desire for the father"; and Sandra Gilbert, in "Life's Empty Pack" (370–73), a survey of the position of the daughter in literature, says that she virtually always belongs to her father permanently.

The present passage, however, follows ALP's violation back through an infinite regress: "Two lads in scoutsch breeches went through her before that, Barefoot Burn and Wallowme Wade . . ." (*FW* 204.5–7). These may be two boys who waded barefoot through ALP when she was only a small rivulet, or two boys who played sexual games with her when she was a child. "Went through" sounds like penetration, but the boys wear breeches. A student of mine, Anne-Marie Flanagan, took a tough feminist view of this passage by emphasizing that Joyce seemed to delight in defiling his heroine. He is susceptible to such humor, but as I see it, he takes little delight in these competitors. His aim is to show that the prevailing model of woman's purity is always already defiled, no matter how innocent she may be.

In *Hamlet* Laertes tells Ophelia, "The chariest maid is prodigal enough / If she unmask her beauty to the moon" (1.3.36–37). Laertes is a voice of convention in the play, and these lines, according to the Arden notes, appear in quotes in the Second Quarto, suggesting that they were a well-known formula at the time. Such a rigid standard of purity makes every woman blamable, and there turn out to be levels of violation before ALP's childhood abuse, levels that suggest infancy.

A cygnet is a young swan, and when Anna was "too frail to flirt with a cygnet's plume" (*FW* 204.11), she was licked by a hound while urinating. But the level before this was the most serious:

but first of all, worst of all, the wiggly livvly, she sideslipped out by a gap in the Devil's glen . . . and, feefee fiefie, fell over a spillway before she found her stride and lay and wriggled in all the stagnant black pools of rainy under a

fallow coo and she laughed innocefree with her limbs aloft and a whole drove
of maiden hawthorns blushing and looking askance upon her. (*FW* 204.14–20)

A good example of how Joyce is always finding new ways to make
language expressive is the phrase "feefee fiefie," which edges up to
"fell." This is the image of brimming water licking at the edge before
going over, and it also carries erotic overtones through the name "Fifi"
and the sexy attitude of defiance. What makes this ALP's worst offense
is that it breaks out of the ordained limits of woman's role, slipping out
of a gap and falling over a spillway. This is what Lacan calls the *jouissance* of the woman that "goes beyond" (*FS* 147). He implies both
overflow and Irigaray's idea of woman's pleasure outside genital orgasm. The "fallow coo" the toddler wriggled under in a series of pools
was a "cow" in the earliest manuscript (*JJA* 48.54), so it is a cow who
is not pregnant, with an overtone of "fellow." "Coo" may also refer to
a soothing sound made by a bird, a parent, or the infant herself, a coo
that made the baby squirm with pleasure. But the cow seems more
substantial here, although there is a puzzle as to how one cow could
extend over "all the . . . pools" little Anna wriggles in. The solution is
that the cow is Nut, the Egyptian sky goddess, who often took the form
of a cow (Ions 49), and whom ALP later identifies as her mother (*FW*
627.8–9). On this level, Anna's primal sin is a communion with her
mother in the Imaginary order of feeling that the father's Symbolic order of language has to break up.

Joyce found value in the interfeminine eroticism of a dream his wife
had of making love to a cow. In 1916 he recorded a series of Nora's
dreams and interpreted them. Here is the text of his transcription of
one of them:

> Lying alone on a hill
> A herd of silver cows
> A cow speaks, making love
> A mountain torrent
> Eileen [Joyce's sister] appears
> The cow has died of its love (*JJ* 437)

Interpreting this dream, Joyce says it shows

a freedom from conventional ideas . . . by the fact that she feels no repulsion at
being made love to by a female beast. . . . Here there is no fear either of goring
or of pregnancy. An experience [love with the cow] more in life and therefore
not to be avoided. Eileen appears as a messenger of those secret tidings which
only women bear to women and the silver mountain torrent, a precious and

wild element, accompanies the secrecy of her messages with the music of romance. (*JJ* 437)

Joyce expresses here a strong recognition of the beauty of the womanly
world of feeling beyond men. The last line of the dream suggests that
Nora laments the loss of the feminine love of infancy.

In ALP's earliest scene, the hawthorns are as female as the cow, so
the scene is entirely feminine in its preoedipal polymorphousness. It is
the kind of pleasure that Irigaray says the patriarchal order suppresses
in women, and this is why the washers, whose conventional views are
saturated with male-oriented attitudes, find it the most objectionable.
Anna can never be enclosed by the phallic economy because she has a
joy that precedes the imposition of gender, but she is finally not allowed to be herself.

The washers are in fact divided into active and passive, since Quickenough usually does the telling, while Doddpebble asks. They are also
divided between Mrs. and Miss. As the boundaries that try to hem
Anna in, they embody the polarity of the traditional gender system in
opposition to her undifferentiated flow. We will see that their different
natures lead to different fates.

ALP's primal pleasure, which these limits oppose, is especially pro-
voking to the male system because it precedes and excludes men:
"where the hand of man has never set foot" (*FW* 203.15). A woman is
attractive to Joyce because she has this magic desire that the man can
never know. And Joyce is drawn continually to the image of the desirable woman in her undifferentiated youth when she played with girl
friends, especially when they dressed as boys. The escape of the
woman from boundaries is seen as the source of creative vitality.

LOST GIFTS

Anna's main action in this chapter is to distribute gifts from her bag to
everyone to counteract the attacks directed at HCE. This dissemination
is an extension of the image of the stream divided by sex. She is said to
give presents to "a thousand and one" of her children (*FW* 210.5). The
Irish anarchist bag of streaming, or "culdee sacco of wabash" (*FW*
210.1), from which her gifts come is the gaping vagina of the Celtic fertility goddess called Sheela-na-gig. Henke (181) refers to ALP's bag as
both a womb and a worksack. Her three pages of gifts (*FW* 210–12),
some of them frightening, are the lives and deaths fated to everyone.
Joyce wrote to Weaver on 7 March 1924, "Her Pandora's box contains

the ills flesh is heir to" (*Letters I* 213). Of course, the gift that starts the trouble is always woman's gift, life. Aïda Yared wrote me that if ALP's "furzeborn sons" (*FW* 210.4) are firstborn, then she not only had them in the fields, but had each by a different father. But her promiscuity may be ubiquity: if all communication is based on love, and the giving of love is feminine, then the reason Anna writes the letter/*Wake* is that every moment of articulation or consciousness, every waking moment anyone has, is given by femininity.

The main emphasis here, however, ends up being on how Anna's gifts get scattered, with the implication that most of the love women give to the world is lost, is ignored, or comes to no good. When Dodd-pebble asks where all ALP's children are now, Quickenough replies, "some here, more no more, more again lost alla stranger" (*FW* 213.31–32). One strong image of her proliferation, the nursery riddle "As I Was Going to St. Ives," turns out to be more ironic than has been seen. The washers say of HCE, "Hadn't he seven dams to wive him? And every dam had her seven crutches. And every crutch had its seven hues. And each hue had a differing cry" (*FW* 215.15–17). The original riddle, as cited by Iona and Peter Opie, ends with a twist:

> As I was going to St. Ives,
> I met a man with seven wives,
> Each wife had seven sacks,
> Each sack had seven cats,
> Each cat had seven kits:
> Kits, cats, sacks, and wives,
> How many were there going to St. Ives?

The Opies (377) say that the correct answer may be either one or none. The only person in the riddle definitely going to St. Ives is the speaker, so all of the feminine multiplicity in the verses is only a distraction, is going nowhere. Similarly, ALP's largess, while it may be productive in some instances, is largely dissipated without positive results; and there are indications that most of her love is wasted because of the way the world is culturally organized.

The lives of the people among whom these gifts have gone astray are filled with complaints, which are heard bouncing over and over against the banks of the river. (McHugh says *bank* is *Ufer* in German and *sponda* in Italian.) "Mezha, didn't you hear it a deluge of times, ufer and ufer, respund to spond? You deed, you deed! I need, I need!" (*FW* 214.7–9). Everyone is blaming and everyone is asking for more.

One of the gifts that goes astray is "scruboak beads for beatified

Biddy" (FW 210.29), which gives an immediate impression of rosary beads for an elderly religious woman. Biddy appears often in the *Wake* in many forms, making her a complex figure in a book in which every character is a recurring and changing group of letters. As Biddy O'Brien, she's the woman who praises the corpse in the song "Finnegans Wake"; and as Biddy Doran, she's the hen who gathers the fragments of ALP's letter. In the largest sense, she's the housekeeper Kate, who is often the old form of ALP.

It may seem strange that Kate is both the washerwomen who frame the narrative and Biddy, whom they speak of; but Joyce delights in this kind of construction, which appears whenever HCE dreams about himself. In fact, HCE sometimes dreams about himself dreaming about himself, as at the start of chapter 4 (FW 75). To use the dual-gender pronouns Joyce invented in the "Circe" episode of *Ulysses*,[3] it may not be possible to see a person accurately without seeing hrim as a dream of shis parents or as shis own dream.

In the gifts passage, Biddy is mainly Saint Bridget or Saint Bride, the female patron saint of Ireland, who established a religious community in 490 at Kildare, which means "church of the oak." Glasheen says that Brigid was an Irish goddess of fertility and poetry who was chastened and Christianized to become Saint Bridget, the patroness of consecrated virgins. The transition illustrates the contrast between the vitality of women in pagan Irish literature and their repression by Christianity.

The text focuses on one straying part of Biddy's gift: "And one of Biddy's beads went bobbing till she rounded up lost histereve with a marigold and a cobbler's candle in a side strain of a main drain of a manzinahurries off Bachelor's Walk" (FW 213.36–214.3). The notes on this passage by C. K. Ogden, which McHugh cites as supervised by Joyce, say that it refers to a "person being given a high place in the church after death." So on this level Biddy's bead's candle is religious and her marigold is a window. Though she is exalted, she is dead. Ogden also says that a "man's in a hurry" is a place for making water. So the biddybead or beady is debased as well as being exalted, in a side urinal as well as a side altar. This corresponds to the familiar Catholic polarized image of woman as sacred and vile. In this position, in which she ended up the last time she became hysterical, she sits out and sums up a history of woman's being lost. She can speak for the alienation of the lost history of Eve only as long as she is decentered in a side strain.

Like the prostitute at the end of the second chapter of *Portrait*, or the confessor at the end of the third, beady is in a little compartment where men in a hurry go to relieve themselves. Her woman's bypath is aside from the main activity of the world, which centers on looking like an independent man, and so is called "Bachelor's Walk." Many women are fixed in the position of being pit stops for men.

The combination of exaltation and debasement imposed on women appears in a famous line from Joyce's recording: "Lord help you, Maria, full of grease, the load is with me!" (FW 214.18–19). By reading this line so as to accent "me," Joyce makes it a statement that the other one is not washing her share of the clothes. But the load of wash here stands for a series of burdens beyond housework that are imposed on women as represented by Mary: the lord, childbearing, and the woman's quality that is emphasized, grace.

Mary's grace is explained in the "Nausicaa" episode of Ulysses, where the men in the chapel are heard praying to the Virgin in the background while Gerty MacDowell exposes herself to Bloom. The men take comfort from Saint Bernard's doctrine that no one who sincerely prays to the Virgin will ever be abandoned by her (U 13.379–80). This is an attitude every Christian woman is responsible for (and other cultures are parallel): no matter how a man may sin, if he repents she must forgive him or her womanhood may be questioned. Kristeva shows in "Stabat Mater" how the image of the Virgin is used to harness women to lives of pain and self-sacrifice that serve the social machinery of the family. This is woman's central grace, and it is also grease because it acts as a lubricant that allows man to screw her easily.

The subversive power of Joyce's lines depends on the common pattern among Catholics of reciting "Hail, Mary, full of grace. / The Lord is with thee." Such recitation may be spoiled for anyone who remembers Joyce's substitution of "grease" for "grace." This is a pointed example of how the Wake's "root language" (FW 424.17) is designed to constantly root out ordinary language (language that gives orders) and the structures it supports.

DECLINE AND RECOGNITION

On this page (214) the washers show how their gifts have gone astray by declining into accusations, complaints, and defensiveness. Doddpebble asks Quickenough, "Were you lifting your elbow, tell us, glazy cheeks, in Conway's Carrigacurra canteen?" (FW 214.20–21), which refers to drinking, and perhaps also to erotic posing. Quickenough retorts, "Was I what, hobbledehips?" She goes on to say that Doddpebble "won" her limp from soldiers "when Collars and Cuffs was heir to the town and your slur gave the stink to Carlow" (*FW* 214.28–30). The word *slur*, according to Skeat, originally meant "to trail in mud," and Doddpebble's slur is supposed to smell as far as Carlow, which is some forty miles from Dublin.

At this point I will give a different spin to the phrase "Collars and Cuffs" than I gave it earlier, and one becomes aware of an important function of the *Wake* when one sees how completely one meaning of a given unit can oppose another, for the book is constantly taking apart the semantic basis of "reality." Collars and cuffs stand for military uniforms, in which they are prominent. *Ulysses* makes it clear that Dublin, as a colonial capital, had an enormous red light district, the main purpose of which was to entertain occupying British troops and the upper classes they supported.

The prostitution of Dublin's women was an extension of the general historical principle that the conqueror has a right to the women of the conquered, with men's competition deciding women's fates. When HCE raped ALP, she was "Sabrine asthore" (*FW* 197.21). This is not only Sabrina, the spirit of the Severn River, a character in Milton's "Comus," taken ashore, but also the Sabine women, who were raped by their conquerors in Roman history. As Yared put it to me, this use of women as booty is the bitter underside of Dryden's line noted earlier, "None but the brave deserve the fair." A version of this is considered (though rejected) as the name of the place where ALP lost her virginity (*FW* 203.10–11), and it was in such a context that Doddpebble was broken or infected so badly that she never recovered. This makes it all the more ironic that her sister in hardship accuses her of having earned ("won") her injury by being a slut.

Those who are most victimized by ideology are often its truest believers. Faulkner saw this pattern in Emily Grierson's attachment to her brutal father in "A Rose for Emily": "with nothing left, she would have to cling to that which had robbed her, as people will." Joyce saw it reflected by the tendency of women to support the Catholic Church, though a woman could see it in the devotion of men to warfare. For Joyce, opposition to the Church was on the side of support for the liberation of women.

Though she has been mistreated horribly by men, Doddpebble continues to search for signs of a male figure, mainly HCE, who she hopes will bring relief from the washers' misery. She turns from Quickenough's charge to say, "Holy Scamander, I sar it again!" (*FW* 214.30). Quickenough responds that it is only "them four old codgers"—only the decrepit world of male authority, only the Evangelists, who appear as four old men in the *Wake*, and not their subject. But Doddpebble continues to hope for a redeeming man who will be a beacon to her (Poolbeg lighthouse), and perhaps also an exhibitionist: "Is that the Poolbeg flasher beyant, pharphar . . . or a glow I behold within a hedge or my Garry come home from the Indes?" (*FW* 215.1–3).

Now there is a change of tone toward emotionality that seems to reflect Quickenough's pity for Doddpebble's delusion. Call it compassion, for Quickenough is not free from the delusion herself, and what surfaces is passion. Continuing to urge restraint, Quickenough says, "Wait till the honeying of the lune, love!" (*FW* 215.3–4). This refers primarily to HCE, who was called *"my maymoon's honey"* in ALP's song (*FW* 201.10); but the transformation of the phrase brings in many other feelings attached to the dreamed-of return, feelings that go beyond HCE.

In early manuscripts, "the honeying of the lune" was "the rising of the moon" (*JJA* 48.97), and this level remains present. It points toward an increase in visibility, but it also generates a political aspect to which I will return. The final version probably refers to the "honey of generation" in Yeats's "Among School Children," and to death and rebirth conceived of as a lunar cycle. Yeats, whose esoteric symbols are parodied in the *Wake*, notes that his honey is based on a concept of Porphyry, a Neoplatonist Joyce mentions (*FW* 100.17, 264 n. 3), and that this honey is a drug that destroys before birth the recollection of prenatal freedom (Yeats 597). So Quickenough seems to advise Doddpebble to await relief from their past life, and to suggest in this paragraph a longing for death.

The Joyce-sponsored notes present the next line—"Die eve, little eve, die!"—as a refrain from a children's game. A similar refrain passes through Leopold Bloom's mind, which associates it with pathos: "Ruin them. Wreck their lives. Then build them cubicles to end their days in. Hushaby. Lullaby. Die, dog. Little dog, die" (*U* 11.1019). For the washers, if Eve dies, the traditional position of woman will be left behind; so the line probably expresses exasperation with those pitiful dreams of Prince Charming. On the level on which these are voices within Kate, part of her is fed up with another part; but the strong feeling of the line suggests that it is also deeply involved in a dream she cannot shake off, a role that grasps her.

The Ogden notes (McHugh 215) explain the next line, "We see that wonder in your eye," by saying, "Strange things are seen in the eyes of persons on the point of death." To look into a dying person's eyes is an extreme of intimacy, and "We see that wonder in your eye" is also erotic—though the plural of the first pronoun is curious. It may show that both women are seeing each other's *Liebestod* together. Death as a sexual act that reveals naked extremity is expressed strongly in Sharon Olds's poems about her dying father in *The Father*.

The sexuality of death is bisexual in that there is no gender distinction: a man watching a loved one die can play the role of a woman, as is indicated by tears. That the suffering shared by the washers unites them intensely is shown by their language: ". . . love! . . . We'll meet again, we'll part once more" (*FW* 215.4–5). Possibly addressing her by an affectionate nickname and certainly showing emotional urgency, Doddpebble says to Quickenough, "Forgivemequick" (*FW* 215.7); and Quickenough replies, "forgetmenot" (*FW* 215.7–8). As they disintegrate, the bond between the two women surges to reveal an underlying homoerotism. Though they intermittently relapse into banter after this paragraph, and they lose contact, a deep level of womanly feeling has emerged that cannot be contained by social and sexual conventions.

The stirring of such feeling, which is the heaving of the water, is linked to political uprising by the submerged but potent reference to "The Rising of the Moon," a familiar ballad:

> O, then, tell me, Shawn O'Farrell,
>   Where the gathering is to be.
> In the old spot by the river
>   Right well known to you and me!
>
> One word more, for signal token,
>   Whistle up the marching tune,
> With your pike upon your shoulder
>   At the rising of the moon.
>   (Harrington 60)

The lines that follow "Wait till the honeying of the lune, love!" suggest such a conspiratorial meeting by the river as well as a romantic assignation (and honeymoon): "We'll meet again. . . . The spot I'll seek if the hour you'll find" (*FW* 215.4–5). In Lady Gregory's well-known play *The Rising of the Moon* (1907), which quotes the lines cited above, the awaited revolutionary get-together is equated with the overturning of all hierarchy and the shifting of all identity: "when the small rise up and the big fall down . . . when we all change places at the rising . . . of the Moon" (Harrington 62; first ellipsis Gregory's). This apocalyptic imagery may be linked to the idea of death as a vision of passing to a better world.

The absorption in death suggested by urging Eve to die and seeing that wonder in her eye involves a rejection of life, and such a rejection, as a denial of the existing order, is crucial to revolution. The serious rebel has to put revolutionary immortality before life in its known state. Through the sense of farewell that the washers are excited by here, they carry each other to the limit of life and beyond. This transfiguration prefigures Anna's turn against the world of the father at the end of the *Wake*.

To separate the drive that exalts this pair for this moment into erotic, deathly, or political components is to take a side for the whole. To assume that the erotic can ever be free of the political or that the political can escape the erotic or that death can ever be conceived of as free of life (which includes the erotic and the political) is to assume that any one of these three can be known by dismembering it. The women in this crisis of expiration realize the impulse on all of its levels, feeling the whole flow rather than merely a side of it.

The oppositions that contain the flow ossify to tree and stone as the voice of the widening river takes over in a pattern parallel to the end of the book. On the level within Kate, the oppositions imposed on her by society dissolve, and her younger, more vital womanhood (ALP) swells within her as she goes to sleep. The last coherent paragraph (*FW* 215.12–30) overthrows convention and patriarchy as it criticizes polar sexual roles and hegemonic marriage, hails ALP's dissemination (the St. Ives material is not entirely ironic), and focuses, as the *Wake* often does, on HCE's bisexuality.

HCE is seen here and elsewhere as an unjust imperialist in his relation to Anna: "He married his markets, cheap by foul, I know, like any Etrurian Catholic Heathen . . ." (*FW* 215.19–20). The degrading nature of his rule is shown by rendering "cheek by jowl" as "cheap by foul," indicating that his closeness is a matter of taking advantage, just as imperialist explores his markets for the purpose of exploiting them. And his gender is questioned in this paragraph, which refers to both HCE and ALP as "queer" (*FW* 215.12–13).

Just as Stephen demonstrated in "Scylla and Charybdis" that Shakespeare's manhood was a denial of lack of manhood, the *Wake* shows phallic authority as inherently false—in this case by going back before the phallus. At the very first creation of the boy's being, he is the passive partner: "But at milkidmass who was the spouse? Then all that was was fair. Tys Elvenland!" (*FW* 215.21–22). In the ideal situation of nursing (a mass of milk for the kid), he was controlled by a woman, and his subsequent life was a decline from this enchantment.

The paragraph goes on, "Teems of times and happy returns. The seim anew. Ordovico or viricordo. Anna was, Livia is, Plurabelle's to be" (*FW* 215.22–24). HCE's happiest times in later life came when he was again passive with a woman, and so Anna is hailed as a deity. Henke (183) points out that the washers turn away from male authority and hail a series of sacred females in the last pages of this chapter, including Maria, "marthared mary allacook" (*FW* 214.23), who sounds like a provider of food, and "Icis on us" (*FW* 214.31). Passages invoking Anna as deity recur in the *Wake*, most notably at the start of chapter 5: "In the name of Annah the Allmaziful, the Everliving, the Bringer of Plurabilities, haloed be her eve, her singtime sung, her rill be run, unhemmed as it is uneven!" (*FW* 104.1–3). As a version of God, Anna opposes his unity and restriction with boundless multiplicity. Instead of a kingdom, she aims at a singtime, the song of dawn.

The washers use the nursing image to realize that HCE is feminine: "He had buckgoat paps on him, soft ones for orphans. Ho, Lord! Twins of his bosom. Lord save us! And ho! Hey? What all men. Hot? His tittering daughters of. Whawk?" (*FW* 215.27–30). McHugh's notes tell us that there was a pagan adoption ceremony of sucking male paps and that Saint Patrick refused to submit to it, indicating a contrast between pagans who had a more open view of gender and a Christian who was dogmatically male. "What all men" refers to the fact that all men have nipples, which are one referent of "Twins of his bosom." The word "Hot?" continues the question by sounding like the German *hat*, "has," as well as suggesting that there may be something exciting about those male nipples. Questions like "Hot?" and "Hey?" are poking fun at the old man.[4]

In fact, men have a certain ability to nurse. Once my wife was shopping and my infant daughter woke, was hungry, and started crying. After she got quite frantic, I gave her my breast, and it worked in that it quieted her down. She soon realized there was no milk and got frustrated, but I was able to hold her until Barbara got back. This is an example of how marriage, insofar as it works, causes men and women to mix genders, or people of the same gender to mix characteristics.

The male breast is a sort of inferior version of the female one, in a reversal of Freud's tendency to see the clitoris as an inferior penis, and the washers find the image uproarious, as we can hear in Joyce's reading of "Ho, Lord!" The line "And ho! Hey?" (which is the second of five *ho*'s here) recurs at the end of the book as "Ho hang! Hang ho!" (627.31). In both cases it is a shouting of exultation of women excited by their freedom. Timothy Martin (217) recognizes the cry of Wagner's

Valkyries here, and there is also a reference to the Hoang Ho, a river with a great tendency to overflow.

The tittering daughters are laughing at their father's femininity, and their laughter is central to the hitherandthithering waters of ALP. Her uncontrollable multivalence now swells to overwhelm all coherence. Perhaps Kate sinks into the mother within her as she sleeps, but then what she sinks into is pure, dynamic creativity.

The washers try to keep their polarities active in discourse: "Ho, talk save us!" (FW 215.34). But with the breakdown of polarities, communication becomes impossible: "Can't hear with bawk of bats, all thim liffeying waters of" (215.33). The waters of night and the night sounds of chattering bats and mice drown out sense and consciousness as ALP passes the ossified opposition of tree and stone, now turned monumental. The *Wake* portrays all cities as "Allalivial, allalluvial!" (FW 213.31) because they pile up at the edges of rivers; but inside the river is the source of life and the productive flow of which all civilizations are deposits. Joyce develops indications that the rivering waters carry the potential of a new world on the other side of this one.

4

Afric Anna

Joyce's Multiracial Heroine

Vielo Anna, high life! Sing us a sula . . .

—*Finnegans Wake*

It is the trope of our times to locate the question of culture in the realm of the *beyond*.

—Homi Bhabha

BEYOND AND BETWEEN

ALP is connected to the non-Western world because women are linked to the beyond of knowledge. The area beyond rational control has often been represented by the unknown parts of the planet, and this construction entails both debasement and potential, the unknown having both lower and higher aspects, being both frightening and attractive. Both women and non-Westerners have historically been adjoined to the space outside the Symbolic order or linguistic structure of established civilization; and this displacement has defined their situations both negatively and positively, in terms of both limitations they are afflicted by and possibilities they can build on.

Most of the continuous characters of the *Wake* pass through multiple racial identities, but great emphasis is placed on imagery that represents Anna as being nonwhite, and especially from Africa. She is of course not exclusively African, but it can be said that the mix of her identities is predominantly Afro-Irish. As Lynda M. Hill points out, she is a hybrid, exemplifying Homi Bhabha's (1–2) theory of hybridity by occupying the " 'in between' spaces" that contain the process of exchange between Europe and the postcolonial world.

54

As a woman, ALP is partly within the patriarchal Symbolic order that claims the title of Civilization. This is the part of her that allows her to appear in one particular language, usually English. She is also in the Symbolic order insofar as she appears clearly in any other language, even Kiswahili. The part of woman that appears outside of the Symbolic order in the beyond is her otherly side. Kiswahili represents this beyond insofar as it appears in the text as an obscurity, something outside known words. It is easy to see the importance of this side in the *Wake*. Her vitality as a woman lies in the in-between, the interaction between her European and non-European sides. This corresponds to Showalter's (201–2) well-known observation that woman's writing is double-voiced, speaking for both the dominant masculine culture and the suppressed feminine one. My present purpose, however, is mainly to prove that Anna's non-Western side is a leading function, crucial to what she stands for.

There are, to be sure, counterindications to the predominance of ALP's African side. For example, she has red hair: "saffron strumans [human streams] of hair . . . deepdark and ample like this red bog at sundown" (*FW* 203.24–25). But this in itself need not keep her from a strong African identity: I once attended a lecture by Malcolm X, and he had bright red hair. If particular physical details of ALP go against her negritude, her attributes are far from consistent: at times she is a hen. Nevertheless, her African features proliferate as central determinants of her role.

The most serious obstacle to these determinants is the way in which Anna often seems to be integrated into a community that often seems Irish, at a time before such integration was feasible. But then the location of her culture often changes identity, and she turns out to be alienated from her community for reasons that involve the conjunction of her womanliness and her Africanism. I use this last word as Toni Morrison does in *Playing in the Dark*; it serves to remind us that Joyce's view of Africa is necessarily European. (Perhaps I should also refer to Joyce's feminism as "womanism," but I think he shows more understanding of women than of Africans.) Joyce had little access to views of Africans that were not stereotypes, but he marshalled his opaque images of people of color so as to evoke a real opposition. I will show that at the end of the *Wake* Anna concludes that she never fit into the patriarchal Irish community at all, and decides to go back to the people she belongs to. These people are women, and the two of them who are identified correspond to the Nile and the Amazon.

When Joyce had *Anna Livia Plurabelle* published separately in 1928, he had the chapter bound "in a tea-colored cover because the Liffey was the color of tea" (*JJ* 603n), and there are continual indications throughout the *Wake* that ALP's skin is dark. The narrator of the story of the Mookse and the Gripes in chapter 6 says of the woman who gathers up the fallen Mookse's body, "I believe she was a Black . . ." (*FW* 158.26).[1] Since the women who gather the bodies here correspond to the washers, this woman is an aspect of ALP. As Hill points out, ALP is introduced before her chapter as "our turfbrown mummy" (*FW* 194.22). Within "ALP" she is referred to as "Duodecimoroon" (*FW* 207.25–26), which means she is one-twelfth Negro.

In fact, as Barbara Lonnquist notes, *anna* is a term used to describe racial mixing in India. The *OED* explains that *ana* is Hindustani for one-sixteenth. The word is most often used for money, an anna being one-sixteenth of a rupee, and the *Wake* uses it in this sense (*FW* 170.1). But it is also used for fractions of race, so that the *OED* says that a quadroon is referred to as "four annas of dark blood."

Anna is described in the chapter in which she makes love to HCE as having a "Nubian shine" (*FW* 559.28). HCE remembers her complexion in these terms: "the swarthy searchall's face on her, with handewers and groinscrubbers and a carrycam to teaze her tussy out, the brown but combly . . ." (*FW* 550.18–20). The last line, while it refers to her hair on one level (McHugh says "carrycam" includes "currycomb"), also refers to the Song of Solomon: "I am black but comely" (1.5).

STEREOTYPYGIA

The tradition that links women to Africans is quite extensive, and includes not only a progressive wing that focuses on the need for liberation in both groups, but a lower level with racist/sexist sources that connects both to uncontrolled physical desire. Sander L. Gilman, in "Black Bodies, White Bodies," examines images of African women and prostitutes in nineteenth-century Europe. He shows that both were seen by scientists as having exaggerated sexual parts, particularly enlarged buttocks and labia. These features were taken as indications that sexually active women and Africans were genetically inferior, and even a lower species (Gilman 228–40). Thus woman's unleashed sexuality was widely linked to African identity.

As Gilman (256–57) points out, Freud is probably influenced by this tradition when in his monograph *The Question of Lay Analysis* (212) he refers to woman's sexuality as the "dark continent" of psychology, though his primary meaning is that it cannot be understood. The tradition may also be reflected by Molly Bloom's deep memories of Gibraltar. Near the lower tip of Spain, Gibraltar is south of Algiers and Tunis, and Molly associates its Moorish atmosphere with youthful passion.

Molly identifies her sexuality as the dark part of her body by playing with a line from the song "Goodbye" (Gifford and Seidman 612). Her version of the original line is "kiss me straight on the brow and part," but she changes the last four words to "my brown part" (U 18.275–76).

If the bottom of Europe is a substratum of Molly's womanhood, there is a level on which ALP's African aspect stands for the fact that all Europeans bear Africa within them because Africa is the origin of civilization. Moreover, most Europeans bear African blood, and Joyce refers to the Irish as a mixture of light (Scandinavian) and dark (Spanish) peoples: "Mearmerge two races, swete and brack" (FW 17.23). Here 'white' and 'black' are almost as prominent as fresh and salt water. For Joyce any—or almost any—nation is a mixture: "It is the same told of all. Many. Miscegenations on miscegenations" (FW 18.19–20).

While the African component of ALP may be shared by most Europeans, it does embody the stereotypical bonding of female sexuality to Africanism. And while Joyce intends this fusion of sexism and racism to liberate through honesty, it cannot avoid being implicated in retrograde elements woven into the cultural system. Joyce does not want to limit himself to a critical or external view of his culture, powerful though that view may be in his work. He represents the multiple voices of culture in a living, dialogic way so that insight and folly mingle. Rather than pretend that desire can be made rational, it may be more useful to see how desire is tangled in and built on cultural errors.

In the Lesson chapter (II.2), ALP's power over men is attributed to mumbo jumbo. This phrase, made popular in Joyce's time by Vachel Lindsay's "The Congo," is a white version of a name for an African spiritual force.[2] The text reads, "She wins them by wons, a haul hectoendecate [111] for mangay mumbo jumbjubes tak mutts and jeffs . . ." (FW 273.16–18). Jujubes were associated in Ulysses with "jujuby women" (U 15.4123), and especially with Molly's "Full gluey woman's lips" (U 4.450) or "gumjelly lips" (U 8.909). So the "jumbjubes" ALP uses to win men are lips whose thickness seems to be flowering for men, "mangay"—and lips like mangoes.

"Celtiberian" soldiers, who represent the dark side of the Irish "race," are described as being "drawn toowards their Bellona's Black Bottom" (FW 78.30), and while the last two words refer to a dance, they also link feminine attraction to the African. This is not the only indication of ALP's steatopygia, which is suggested by a phrase already quoted, "teaze her tussy out" (FW 550.20). Issy is referred to as "the totter of Blackarss" (FW 251.11), which implies that her rear end and her mother's practice black magic by swaying.

One of the main images of the center of ALP's attractiveness is heliotrope, the flower that bends to the sun. Sailer says it stands for "The female genital environment" (72). In the Children's Games chapter, Shem struggles to guess the color of Issy's drawers, which are heliotrope. One anagram of heliotrope presented here is "Ethiaop lore" (FW 223.28), which suggests that Issy's hidden parts embody African lessons.

ALP's vagina is referred to as "her sheba sheath" (FW 198.3), linking it to the exotic Queen of Sheba. The word *exotic* contains within itself the bond between the Third World and sexuality. The Queen, who comes from southern Arabia, is portrayed as a temptress in Flaubert's *Temptation of St. Anthony* (chapter 2) and in Yeats's "Solomon to Sheba," which calls her "dusky."

The main source for ALP's initials is the most colossal image of a woman's sex organ in anglophone literature, an orientalist image of the non-Western world:

> Where Alph, the sacred river, ran
> Through caverns measureless to man
> Down to a sunless sea.
> So twice five miles of fertile ground
> With walls and towers were girdled round:
> And there were gardens bright with
> sinuous rills. . . .

These "twice five miles of fertile ground" that are "girdled round" are represented in the diagram of ALP in the Study chapter (FW 293) (see Figure 1).

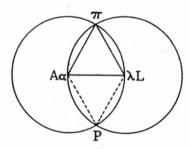

Figure 1. ALP.

There is a good deal more of sexual imagery in "Kubla Khan," including strong images of orgasm:

> And from this chasm, with ceaseless
>   turmoil seething,
> As if the earth in fast thick pants were
>   breathing,
> A mighty fountain momently was forced:
> Amid whose swift half intermitted burst
> Huge fragments vaulted like rebounding
>   hail. . . .

Joyce would have noticed such orgasmic rhythm, and been struck by the combination of orgasm and excretion, though neither Coleridge nor Joyce may ever have seen the rare phenomenon of female ejaculation. In fact, Coleridge probably did not know he was describing a woman's private parts, but Joyce, with his interest in the body as landscape, would have noticed this pattern in "Kubla Khan." What I am most concerned with here, however, is that Coleridge ends up identifying his visionary power with an African girl singing:

> A damsel with a dulcimer
> In a vision once I saw:
> She was an Abyssinian maid,
> And on her dulcimer she played,
> Singing of Mount Abora.
> Could I revive within me
> Her symphony and song,
> To such a deep delight 'twould win me,
> That with music loud and long,
> I would build that dome in air,
> That sunny dome! Those caves of ice!

If he could capture her music, his creative imagination would be absolute. This version of the Other typifies the ways in which the Romantics pioneered the idea that the source of a new dispensation lay outside the logical categories of the West. Shem, the son who is closest to ALP and transcribes the letter, represents the Romantic artist and is described as dark-skinned and associated with the blackness of the ink he writes himself in (FW 177.4, 185.8–186.18, 194.18).

THE OTHER WORLD, OR THE SONG OF AFRICA

The progressive aspect of Joyce's equation of ALP with Africa is highly
developed, and some of his decisive sources take pro-African and
feminist positions. Joyce read a substantial version of the widespread
analogy between women and African slaves in John Stuart Mill's *The
Subjection of Women* (1859), which is named in the "ALP" chapter in
such a way as to make woman parallel to a river: "Mill (J.) *On Woman
with Ditto on the Floss*" (*FW* 213.2). Mill uses the horror of slavery to
intensify his indictment of the mistreatment of women. He says that
when slaves finish work, they go to their own homes, but women have
to stay with their husbands all the time, and while masters are not le-
gally entitled to sexual favors from their slaves, a woman would have
to keep having sex with a husband she hated (Mill 33). Mill (22) says
that slaves may be allowed to maintain their own culture (an optimistic
view), but women are entirely shaped by the culture of men. Like Irigaray, he holds that we do not know what women could be, for we see
them only under the control of men (Mill 23).

Joyce made an effort to relate ALP to African material. She is identified with the Nile as the source of civilization, and there are many
references in the *Wake* to the search for the source of the *Nile*, which
was found in Lake Victoria Nyanza in central Africa in 1862. Glasheen
(209) points out that the original name of the lake, Nyanza, was based
on *anza*, the Bantu word for water, which resembles Anna. By playing on "Noanswa" (*FW* 23.20), Joyce implies that if you look for the
source of ALP, you will find no answer. On the other hand, Vivian
Mercier told Glasheen (209) that *ni h annsa* is an Irish answer to riddles,
and means "not hard," or easy to answer. It seems that the dark
continent could be understood if we could only recover its lost language, but that language may never be extricated from the confusion
of history.

Laurent Milesi cites a letter Joyce wrote to Weaver on 13 May 1927,
which refers to Victoria Nyanza as "the source of the Nile, later supposed to represent" HCE and ALP (*SL* 322); but Milesi (85–86) demonstrates that Joyce also recognizes this source as more female and
complex. Milesi points out that Victoria Nyanza, which is upstream
from or prior to its male equivalent, Albert Nyanza, is the source only
of the White Nile. Because the Nile has several branches, it has "many
disputable sources" (Milesi 85), so that the British imperial claim to
find the source is an imposition of unity on the multiplicity of the African waterscape, as is indicated by formulations like "soorcelossness"

(*FW* 23.19). Milesi (89) also points out that the origin of the Nile corresponds to the origin of ALP's letter, the flow of her discourse.

The eight hundred or more river names in the "ALP" chapter cover the whole world, and Rose and O'Hanlon say that Joyce remarked that "he liked to think how some day way off in Tibet or Somaliland some little boy or girl in reading 'Anna Livia' would be tickled pink to come across the name of his or her home river" (114). If the book covers the world, "ALP" seems to focus on Africa, for I.8 has an especially high concentration of Kiswahili words, with thirty of them listed by McHugh between pages 198 and 209.

Most of these African words refer to desire. Doddpebble, for example, uses four of them in the paragraph that begins "Onon!" as she is explaining why she is so impatient to hear everything about ALP: "That homa fever's winning me wome. If the mahun of the horse but hard me! We'd be bundukiboi meet askarigal" (*FW* 201.23–25). McHugh says that *bunduki, boi,* and *askari* are Kiswahili for "gun," "boy," and "soldier," so one of the main meanings here is that if the man of the house heard her talking about ALP, there'd be a fight. He might also assault her as a centaur—"If the mahun of the horse but hard me!" It is not clear whether he would attack her for being against ALP or for being on her side, but I believe the latter is true, for this passage is preceded by ALP's song, which generally seems sympathetic. The washer's interest in a woman's experience would anger the patriarch.

Doddpebble uses *homa*, the Kiswahili for "fever" to explain her desire to look closely into the motivation of ALP's sexual desire: "why were the vesles vet" (*FW* 201.23). The washer locates in her own womb a fever to return to her home source when she says, "That homa fever's winning me wome." The idea of a heated home source tends to combine woman's body and Africa. Joyce seems to recognize through his appreciation of adolescent lesbian proclivities that there is an early female body, a girl-to-girl intimacy that is evoked by the conspiracy of gossip. It is lost when women enter courtship, marry, and subject themselves to patriarchy. To some extent this myth of the lost childhood feminine body overlaps with the myth of infantile polymorphous perversity that is suppressed by genital sexuality, a myth Norman O. Brown traces through a host of visionaries in *Life against Death*. But the classic geographical locus of the lost adolescent lesbian body is non-Western, for Sappho had her school in Mytilene, a town on the east coast of Lesbos that is located in a bay surrounded on three sides by Turkey. Near this bay is Ephesus, the seat of the pre-Hellenic goddess Diana.

Joyce's conception of the *Wake* included the possibility that the parts of the world that are held under by the establishment would wake to liberate the planet. This downtrodden part of the world has been represented as a woman identified with Asia or Africa. The main Asian model is in Shelley's *Prometheus Unbound*, which the *Wake* identifies with desire as "Promiscuous Omebound" (*FW* 560.1). In this great dramatic poem, Asia, who is identified with the principle of love, joins Prometheus as humanity is released from bondage.

The African model, however, is the one emphasized in my present context, and Joyce may have had the image of Mother Africa waking from oppression in mind when he wrote "ALP." He had read invocations to Africa in the abolitionist Blake, who represented Africa as a woman in his 1792 engraving *Europe supported by Africa & America* (Figure 2). Here Europe is held up in her freedom by Africa and America, who are in symbolic chains.

This is an illustration for Captain J. G. Stedman's *Revolted Negroes of Surinam* (1796), and Blake used many details of this account of the mistreatment of Africans in his prophecy calling for the liberation of women, *Visions of the Daughters of Albion* (1793). The white heroine of the *Visions*, Oothon, is portrayed as a slave in chains. David Erdman (233) points out that in the fourth plate of the *Visions*, "The cold green wave enveloping the chained Oothon is symbolic of the drowning of slaves in passage from Africa." Though he does so in ethnocentric and condescending terms, Blake calls on Africa to awake from its subjugation in "A Song of Liberty," the last section of *The Marriage of Heaven and Hell* (1793), a favorite work of Joyce's: "O African! black African! (go. winged thought widen his forehead.)" (Blake 43, with his punctuation).

The imagery linking Africa to a woman who has been violated and is now awakening would eventually be arranged in more Afrocentric terms in such works as Maya Angelou's poem "Africa" (1975). The last stanza of this poem is not without parallelism to the situation of ALP at the end of the *Wake*, where she seems long to have been in bed but now imagines herself getting up and walking. Cixous says that bed is a place that men want women to be permanently ("Castration" 43), and Molly Bloom, as a sign of her entrapment, is never shown anywhere else.

> Now she is rising
> remember her pain
> remember the losses

her screams loud and vain
remember her riches
her history slain
now she is striding
although she had lain.

If Africa's history is slain, she will have to round "up lost histereve." Joyce dealt with his inability to speak for non-Western or female others in their own "lost" languages by using the biased language available to him parodically to reveal its falseness. After all, members of these excluded groups have a hard time finding a language to speak in that is not corrupted, and Irigaray feels that no such language exists as yet for woman. To assume an authentic language untouched by bias would gloss over the seriousness of the conflict. A problem Morrison emphasizes in white Africanist writers is their pretense that they portray Africans objectively, but Joyce makes no such pretense.

In "ALP" Joyce follows a pattern of linking women to racist images of people of color, as John Lennon, a fan of the *Wake*, does in a song he wrote with Yoko Ono, "Woman Is the Nigger of the World." Anna dresses up in "natural nigger boggers" (*FW* 208.16). "Natural nigger" is probably turn-of-the-century fashion terminology for unbleached fabric, for Gerty MacDowell in *Ulysses* wears a "hat of wideleaved nigger straw contrast" (*U* 13.156). But "natural" also refers to a down-to-earth African American rather than a middle-class one. In his 1928 recording "Kassie Jones, Part 2," Walter "Furry" Lewis sings, "I'm a natural Negro on the road again." The clothing of the natural Negro expresses Anna's tendency to sink to the lower level.

Anna is indelibly African, mainly through her Egyptian mother Nut, and Joyce was aware that from a racist point of view to be part African was to be "black." Yet as a woman who is in between, she is also partly a European who is influenced by and attracted to African culture. On one level ALP in her earthiness, with flowers in her hair and her bangles clicking (*FW* 207.1–7), seems to have the features of a hipster. And Joyce had encountered jazz-age proto-hipsters, whites who imitated blacks, in Paris during the twenties. Ellmann reports that at Joyce's birthday party in 1928 the white intellectual Robert McAlmon sang the blues and danced "on negro themes" (*JJ* 599); and Ruth Bauerle (152) cites Louis Armstrong as a favorite of Joyce's bohemian daughter Lucia. When the men of the town see ALP coming in her wild getup, they suspect that *"ALP has doped!"* (*FW* 209.9).

Figure 2. William Blake, *Europe supported by Africa and America*. Engraved in 1792.

Many feminine features of ALP in her chapter, however, are directly connected to Africa. With regard to her gushes of emotion, one of the washers tells the other to "call a spate a spate" (*FW* 198.19). In her costume Anna is described as "a bushman woman" (*FW* 207.34), which implies not only that she is African, but that she includes both genders. Then she is called "between two ages," which means not only that her age is uncertain, but that the movement of woman toward what she contains within herself carries her beyond existing civilization into a new era.

The washers say of ALP, "Botlettle I thought she'd act that loa" (*FW* 198.22–23). A loa is a Haitian divinity derived from African sources (Gates 5). When the young ALP rises in her own estimation (and estivation) because Michael Arklow kissed her, the beneficial effects of this kiss are described in terms of two African languages, Kiswahili and Bantu (though Swahili is a branch of the Bantu group): "That was kissuahealing with bantur [banter] for balm!" (*FW* 204.3–4).

When Anna goes out with her bag of presents, young people call on her to give them music: "Vielo Anna, high life! Sing us a sula, O, susuria!" (*FW* 209.34–35). They seem to ask for a high life, which student Siphokazi Koyana describes as a west African musical form that originated in the 1950s. "O susuria" includes the German for sweet, *süss*, and the Latin for whisper, *susurrus*, but it also refers to "Oh, Susanna," a minstrel song that features a west African instrument, the banjo. Toni Morrison informs me that *sula*, the title of one of her novels, means "water" in Twi. Therefore Anna is asked, in a west African language spoken in Ghana (which Joyce knew as the Gold Coast), to sing in liquid.

At one point, as McHugh indicates, Joyce combines the names of three rivers (the Limmat, the Negro, and the Plate) with a racist tag (about an African looking in a mirror) to present the image of a black man looking once into a silver field and seeing a limit: "Yssel that the limmat? As El Negro winced when he wonced in La Plate" (*FW* 198.13–14). This use of *limit* may have African American origins, as suggested by Sidney Bechet's 1941 recording "You're the Limit." As the present quote is a reaction to Anna's calling in girls for HCE, it may be that the African is seeing in degeneracy (and racism) the limit of Western civilization.

The imagery of the decline of the West grows prominent toward the end of the chapter, and Spengler is referred to, as "spanglers," in the *Wake* (*FW* 151.9, 521.1).[3] Part IV of the *Wake* generalizes about "The untireties of livesliving" (*FW* 597.7), which may be the process of history:

"there are two signs to turn to, the yest and the ist, the wright side and the wronged side, feeling aslip and waulking up, so an . . ." (*FW* 597.10–12). Here the West is falling asleep, and the East, which has been wronged, is waking up, and may be linked to "an". One of the Eastern terms that follow in this paragraph is "Shavarsanjivana" (*FW* 597.19), which McHugh says is based on *shava sam-jivana*, the Sanskrit for "corpse being restored to life," an image of the East waking that ends with "ana." In III.2 it is predicted that "The west shall shake the east awake" (*FW* 473.22–23).

In "ALP," the washerwomen who represent the opposition between Shem and Shaun that makes up patriarchy start to forget the story of the sons as their polarities harden into inanimacy. Doddpebble asks, "Who were Shem and Shaun the living sons or daughters of?" (*FW* 216.1–2), not even clear about their genders in the final paragraph in which the washers turn into a stone and a tree: "My foos won't moos. I feel as old as yonder elm" (*FW* 215.34–35). But their fates are not equal. The passive Doddpebble simply ossifies into a stone, while Quickenough, who tells Anna's story, passes something on. The artist can reach through to the other side, and see herself reflected in the Other.

Doddpebble perceives her metamorphosis in a dull way: "My ho head halls. I feel as heavy as yonder stone" (*FW* 215.36–216.1). But Quickenough sees herself as a tree in a defamiliarized form by looking into Anna Liffey: "Look, look, the dusk is growing! My branches lofty are taking root. And my cold cher's gone ashley" (*FW* 213.12–14). The last sentence is probably spoken by Doddpebble, but the second interests me most. The notes Joyce sponsored gloss the second sentence as follows: "At this point the woman who is to be turned into a tree sees herself pictured upside down in the water, in the form that she later takes" (McHugh 213).

As her culture loses life, she sees herself reflected in reverse on the face of the waters of night. The significance of Western civilization is now seen in terms of how it appears from outside, from the Other end. Quickenough's perception can be seen from another side, and takes great meaning from the viewpoint of the non-Western world. For the tree image seems to be based on the Katha Upanishad, a philosophical scripture written in Sanskrit around the time of Plato or earlier. Near the end of this Upanishad, after speaking of reincarnation, Yama (Death) says, "The tree of Eternity has its roots in heaven above and its branches reach down to earth" (Mascaro 65). Later on this page it is said that Brahman, the eternal principle that is sought, appears "as remembrance of dreams" or "as reflections in trembling waters."

The clearest reference to the Upanishads in the *Wake* is a version of "up and at 'em": "Upanishadem" (*FW* 303.13). But there seem to be references to *Katha*, which is pronounced as if the *th* were a *t*, and it may be linked to Kate, who is first introduced as "Kathe" (*FW* 8.8), the "janitrix" who presides over the museum of history. Atherton (228) mentions that one of the Sanskrit words in the *Wake* is "katya" (*FW* 40.11), which means "widow," and Kate is identified as a widow (*FW* 79.27). She may be evoked when girls dance "a kathareen round" (*FW* 330.35). This could refer to reincarnation and the water cycle, the movement from rain to stream to ocean to cloud in which ALP is involved, which is suggested by "the kathartic ocean" (*FW* 185.06).

Swami Nikhilinanda (80n) says that the tree image in the Katha Upanishad is based on the banyan tree, whose branches come down to earth and germinate there to start new trees. Joyce's version of the image may be related to a point earlier in this chapter when people hung HCE's picture upside down in disgrace (*FW* 205.27–28). But I believe it reflects a reversal of priorities in the West—a focus on non-Western and feminine sources and subjects in such modernists as Conrad, Stein, Lawrence, Woolf, and Faulkner. The growing importance of women and non-Western writers was to follow.

What was formerly held under must now be lifted up as a prime source of insight, and the branches we lifted to promote our accomplishments must now be sent down to regenerate themselves in reverse on the other side of the new era. This perspective applies both to the relation of the West to the Third World and to the relation of men to women. Hierarchies must be reversed, and we must begin to see things from what Irigaray (9) refers to as the other side of the looking glass.

The mirror reversal that ALP reveals implies that men and women will have to become more like each other, as will the Western and non-Western worlds. Insofar as women and non-Westerners protest and fight, they are likely to take on the technology of male Western politics. Insofar as men and Westerners defend what is unfair and put security above truth, they lose the real virtue of manliness and move toward the protected status of dependents, the traditional status of women and the colonized. Therefore the West should take on the best relational qualities of women and the colonized, and postcolonial people should develop Western rationalism, as they tend to do while denouncing it.

5

Going to the Chapel

MINXING MARRAGE AND MAKING LOOF

If the *Wake* develops analogies between women and the colonized, it also argues that the big cycles of inversion that make up history operate similarly to the small ones of personal life. The kind of reversal discussed above—the leaving behind of established polarities, the confrontation with the Other—must be recognized in our most fundamental and intimate activities. The family relations of the *Wake* serve to delineate such interactions between and within generations and genders. Central to the family is marriage, the continuous sexual relation which involves interchange of self and gender. Joyce, as I will show, defines marriage as the best way to see yourself from the other end, to get to the other side of the mirror. Yet he also defines it as an institution that must be reunderstood and reconstituted.

On the first page of the ALP chapter, the washers accuse HCE of "minxing marrage and making loof" (*FW* 196.36).[1] The charge can be interpreted in many ways, including adultery, or marrying one person and loving another; but I think that the idea of mixing works against this level. This term suggests that the two activities could be combined in one relationship, which might not be a bad thing. Yet HCE seems brutal in this chapter, and I think the real problem is indicated by the combination of marring and making: he confuses the destructive and productive aspects of a relationship. He mixes up the patriarchal ownership involved in marriage, an imposition that mars one's mate, with the creative encounter with the unknown in love, which should be the real basis of marriage. On a less prominent level, loafing or being aloof could be seen as passive behavior opposed to the aggressiveness of marring; so the charge against him would be combining active and passive, which is what the washers accuse him of when they refer to his paps.

The life of any marriage, whether it be official or unofficial, hetero- or homosexual, consists of exchanging with the other continually. This interchange is presented with a different use of "marrage" in part IV of the *Wake* when HCE seems to half wake and find himself next to ALP just before "Dayagreening gains in schlimninging" (*FW* 607.24). McHugh finds references in this line to the Irish *deo-greine*, "spark of the sun," the Swedish *daggryning*, "dawn," and the German *Schlimm*, "evil." So it links dawn to hope, as the last part often does. HCE now finds himself so entangled with his wife that he cannot tell which is which:

That my dig pressed in your dag si. . . . Mees is thees knees. Thi is mi. We have caught oneselves, Sveasmeas, in somes incontigruity coumplegs of heopon-hurrish marrage from whose I most sublumbunate. (*FW* 607.17–21)

Whether or not ALP is really there (for we cannot be sure whether the *Wake* ever passes out of its dream), he feels unable to separate her parts from his own. The situation illustrates a truth of marriage: one is often kidding oneself if one tries to distinguish whether a given feeling, thought, or action comes from oneself or one's mate. Through the other one marries one makes rich contact with the big Other, the idea of otherness against which one defines oneself. As Lacan says, "The Other is, therefore, the locus in which is constituted the I who speaks to him who hears, that which is said by the one being already the reply . . ." (*Écrits* 141).

The details of the HCE passage enact in language the reversal of identity. The spelling of *is* backward turns being around, and the attempt to distinguish his knees from hers leads to a muddle, with "thees," for example, combining mine and yours as *this* and *thee*. "We have caught oneselves" also indicates con-fusion. They are caught in a complex of a couple of legs that mixes contiguity with incongruity.

This "heoponhurrish marrage" is a confusion of genders, partly because when a man opens himself up to intimacy, he becomes "herish." An earlier description of HCE (greatly transformed from a song, as McHugh notes) expresses the tendency of husbands and wives to take on each other's gender characteristics: "when older links lock older hearts then he'll resemble she" (*FW* 135.32–33). HCE feels he must extricate himself from this confusion of genders by sublumbunation. Since *lumbar* means "of the loins" and nates are buttocks, this has the physical meaning of taking one part of the body out from under another. But it also implies that he must sublimate his identity and his gender out of the interaction upon which they are based.

In my article "The Femasculine Obsubject," I argue that masculinity and femininity in the *Wake*, as in Lacan, are formed by separating the masculine subject and the feminine object out of the interplay my title refers to. I also hold that femininity consists of the flow of language while masculinity consists of its fixity. These two sides, "woman formed mobile or man made static" (*FW* 309.21–22), are represented by ALP as a river who keeps going on and HCE as a tower who tries to stand firm in a definite position.

Kristeva holds that masculine discourse cannot exist without feminine, for "the signifying process that constitutes language" must combine the maternal pulsation of the semiotic with the paternal fixation of the symbolic (*Revolution* 24). Jean-Michel Rabaté (154–80) demonstrates that the narrative voice of the dreamer of the *Wake* is usually bisexual. And Joyce included in the beginning of his recording from "ALP" a statement that all speech has to involve masculine and feminine sides: "every telling has a taling and that's the he and the she of it" (*FW* 213.12). The masculine telling is an enumeration of the facts, but a female tail of extra meaning always hangs off the end of every attempt at a cut-and-dry statement. If all discourse requires both genders, it is impossible to separate them, and the poles of gender are nonexistent abstractions, virtual images.

HCE illustrates the folly of trying to isolate the masculine as he perpetually erects his tower. It has no more chance of staying up than a penis, and after it collapses, Anna rescues him. Joyce, then, shares Irigaray's idea that sexual polarity must be passed beyond. But if man must stop trying to extricate himself from the interplay of genders, woman's position is different. Man has generally been allowed to be free of "heoponhurrish marrage," but woman has been compelled to try to find her identity within it. Therefore woman, unlike man, may have to separate herself in order to try to find out what she could be if the male-controlled system were not imposed on her. Even if the main source of development lies in interaction, woman must withdraw from the existing one-sided complex if she is ever to interact with relative equality.

Irigaray (90) says that woman's body is obliterated by male construction that defines her feelings. A primary step woman must take to reclaim her own body is to see that it is occupied by the interchange of genders. Man can visit and leave behind this interchange, this "heoponhurrish marrage," this femasculine obsubject. But woman contains and is contained by it; she is situated in and identified with the chamber in which this interchange takes place. And this chamber is located by society "in a side strain of a main drain of a manzinahurries" (*FW* 214.2–3).

She must reclaim this chamber as her own. Though the separation of the feminine from the masculine may seem impossible because of the existing limits of language, it must be striven for despite terror. ALP finally moves toward making such a separation by carrying her vision of the chamber of womanhood beyond male authority, though she is overwhelmed by fear as she does so. To trace her development in this direction, I will start by examining the presentation throughout the *Wake* of this chamber, which plays a central role. I will also glance at some of the cultural traditions in which this edifice is ensconced.

THE CHAPEL, AND ITS SENSITIVE SAINT

Joyce's analysis of the structure that relates HCE to ALP shows the operation of a lost, mythical, unrecoverable unity. They are involved in a language system that designs them to fuse with each other at the cost of their own identities and genders. The most definite forms of the identities of HCE and ALP lie in the letters that name them, but these letters define them as scattered parts of a sacred edifice that would be formed by their fusion. After all, masculine and feminine, as historical constructs, are built into a system predicated upon their union, though that union is impossible. The construction that unites HCE and ALP constitutes the place where they reside. For as Niall Montgomery (442–44, cited by B. Benstock 85) first pointed out, HCE and ALP combine to form the anna-gram CHAPEL.

This anagram is supposed to sound arbitrary because the structure into which people are inserted as men and women is anything but natural. Nevertheless, there are some appropriate overtones in chapel, including oppressive ones. The word originally referred to a cloak (late Latin *cappa*, see *FW* 606.5) divided between two people. The first chapel was the repository of the cloak of the fourth-century Saint Martin of Tours, which he cut in half to share with a naked beggar. Saint Martin dividing his cloak has been painted by Simone Martini, Domenico Ghirlandaio and his studio, and El Greco.

Chapel originally referred to a place of worship aside from the main church, and it also came to refer to a place of worship for a religion other than the official one. As such it was often used for places where

Catholics prayed in Protestant-ruled Ireland. Therefore the word has a suggestion of displaced or decentered devotion.[2]

One of the descriptive lines given for HCE in the sixth chapter is "the beggars cloak them reclined about his paddystool . . ." (*FW* 130.6). Saint Martin's cloak tends to link itself to the cloak of faith in Swift's *A Tale of a Tub*, which is divided among three sons who represent different versions of Christianity, one of them named Martin (for Luther). Both cloaks may be referred to when the washers speak of "Waterhouse's clogh," though their primary reference is to an actual Dublin clock mentioned in "Two Gallants." Earlier they referred to HCE as "Wasserbourne the waterbaby" (*FW* 198.8), and in a draft this "Wasserbourne" was "Waterhouse" (*JJA* 48.15).

Lacan uses Saint Martin's cloak as part of an argument that to do good always requires self-division (*Ethics* 186, 226–28). When Anna gave her love, she was divided into two channels, and a man who gives his love will also divide his intentions on the fault line between self and other. What the washers say about HCE's "clogh" suggests that he is as divided by his marriage as ALP is, and that this division was caused by society, which is referred to by "they": " 'Tis endless now senne eye or erewhone last saw Waterhouse's clogh. They took it asunder, I hurd thum sigh. When will they reassemble it?" (*FW* 213.15–17). Near the end of the book ALP addresses to HCE her dream of reassembling his "clogh," or getting his *cloghad*, a word for belfry used in Ireland, ticking again. In "Nausicaa," when Bloom, another figure identified with a timepiece, tells Cissy Caffrey that his watch has stopped, she quips that his "waterworks were out of order" (*U* 13.551). Gifford and Seidman point out that "waterworks" was "low slang for urinary organs" (392). Anna tries to stimulate HCE by calling him a lady-killer with an attraction to *le cul*: "One of these fine days, lewdy culler, you must redoform again. Blessed shield Martin! Softly so" (*FW* 624.19–20). Though she appeals to his lust, she wants his new form to be not only more faithful, but softer, more feminine. At the same time, his reunited form is linked to Martin's cloak.

There is a contradiction here between wanting his cloak to be united and wanting him to be softer. Martin would not have been a saint if he hadn't divided his military cloak, so that wishing to unite his cloak is a negation of his nature, a negation that forms a sublime object of religious ideology. The saint is a hero (a phallic role) because he is gentle (feminine), and a similar contradiction is involved in the idea of the gentle/man. The division of the cloak may represent the impossibility of maintaining the unity that constitutes patriarchal faith. In Swift's model, the authority of the church is subject to criticism once it is divided. Thus, the dividing of the cloak, as an extension of Christ's idea that the rich should give their money to the poor, has revolutionary implications that go against the church's authority. Like the phallus, the church demands unity, but never attains it./

The sundering of HCE's "clogh" stands for a basic flaw in HCE's manhood so serious that it is "endless" since anyone has seen him standing tall (FW 213.15). He cannot be a real man until his cloak is reassembled. This dilemma is parallel to the problem of Martin's manhood. Wim Van Mierlo says that late in 1923 Joyce took notes on Margaret Maitland's *Life and Legends of St. Martin of Tours* (1908).[3] He was impressed by the way Martin's monks "held all things in common" (Maitland 44), which made him write "monks bolsh[ies]" (*JJA* 29.110). He may also have noticed the prevalence of homoerotic inclinations in Martin's life, and this subversive ambivalence (linked to revolutionary attitudes in the *Wake*) may have led Joyce to put Martin in a key position. In fact Glasheen (188) thinks that the *Wake* is set on 11 November, Martinmas (see FW 517.33–34).

Martin's father forced him to begin his career as a soldier, but Martin refused to attack (Maitland 9–15). The beggar with whom he divided his cloak is described by Maitland as "a trembling half naked man" in a passage Joyce transcribed (*JJA* 29.110). After this the other soldiers laughed at Martin for going around in half a cloak, but then he had a dream in which the Lord appeared to him in a half cloak (Maitland 13). The emotional scenes that transmit half nakedness from beggar to Martin to Christ (like a purloined letter in a daisy chain?) suggest the prominence of homosexuality, if only latent, in Martin's story. As a bishop he allowed a beggar to get into his secret inner chamber and gave the man his tunic. When the archdeacon arrived, Martin had to conceal the fact that he was naked under his cloak (Maitland 91–92). Martin generally did not allow women to approach him (Maitland 61), and the pagan Roman society in which he grew up may have permitted homosexuality.[4]

One of Martin's duties as bishop was to recruit boys for the monastery. He took Victorius from his parents when the lad was ten, making his mother a nun and his father (who at first thought Martin was joking) a bishop (Maitland 82–85). Martin and Victorius were known to spend their nights together in devotion (Maitland 88). Of another young man who passed away in Martin's community of monks, Joyce noted that Martin found the "soul of this particular / young boy dear" (*JJA* 29.110). He lay down with the body, sent everyone out, and pressed himself against it for hours, after which there was a "gentle quiver," "the beloved boy" revived, and Martin "burst into a cry of praise" (Maitland 34). His procedure here followed a biblical precedent (1 Kings 17.17), but this does not keep it from being an expression of Martin. It may be the most intimate moment in his biography: "In some mysterious manner that he afterward tried to describe, he felt, while his body touched the dead one, that life went out from him into it" (Maitland 33).

The homoerotic undertones in the life of this patriarch reflect the impossibility of maintaining the unity that the phallus stands for. Martin's cloak will never be reunited; and in making Martin's chapel a central symbol of love in the *Wake*, Joyce seems to insist that desire is ambivalent, suppressed, opposed to convention, and unknowable. And the primal sin that defines HCE's personality has plenty of homosexual overtones. Milesi points out that in an early MS version of the incident in the Phoenix Park, HCE's crime—which includes "annoying" soldiers (*FW* 33.26), though more emphasis is placed on spying on women in most versions—is excused by extenuating circumstances, especially an "abnormal S Martin's summer" (Milesi 98). In the final version in I.2, "S Martin's" is changed to "Saint Swithin's" (*FW* 34.28).

In order to give the illusion of patriarchal unity, the division in masculine authority must be hidden by being projected onto females—a projection that puts it outside cognizance, or sanctions its location outside cognizance, by situating it in the unfathomable core of femininity.

The pious Maitland is quite oblivious to Martin's inner sexual ambivalence, and a similar obliteration of women's own inner feelings has prevailed in the world of patriarchal romance, as is indicated by the fate of Isolde's chapel. Chapelizod, where HCE and ALP tend to live, is a suburb of Dublin that is supposed to be the site of this chapel, which functions symbolically as a shrine to ALP's beauty, as represented by her daughter, Issy. But there is no known structure here that claims to be or to locate the actual chapel of Izod (Chart 317); so the edifice on which love is based is lost and apparently unrecoverable. Izod's chapel is the seat of her power in the marginal world she and her mother rule before Tristan comes to draw her into the central world of the oedipal triangle with himself and Mark. This chapel stands for woman's body before male imposition, so it accords with Irigaray's theories that this construct cannot be found. The attempt to locate Izod's chapel runs into a series of alternative versions, including Martin's chapel, whose name it bears.

What would Izod's chapel have been called if it were not subject to the patriarchal term *chapel*? From a deconstructive point of view, the most important thing about this chapel is that it never appears in definite form; and the vital activity of life consists of taking it apart and playing with the pieces. If it holds a place in a structure, this may be only until another one is found, for new structures continually turn up in the *Wake*. But if we want to go beyond the structure history has given us, we must attend to that structure carefully.

The term *chapel* has long been associated with marriage, as it is in the *Wake*: "endurses his doom at chapel exit" (*FW* 127.28–29). Love links our couple to the chapel not only because love is lit up by the creative sources religion celebrates, but because it is shadowed by the inhumanity of religion, its deathly air of sacrifice. In order to combine in this chapel, HCE and ALP would have to be dismembered, for his *E* would have to be separated from *CH*, and her *L* would be separated from *AP*. As signifiers they are intertwined, and another anagram for them is PLEACH, or "interlace."

THE CAVE

I believe that one of the main referents of the central term *chapel* in the *Wake* is the Cave of Lovers in Gottfried von Strassburg's *Tristan* (1210). Admittedly, the cave does not appear in the versions of the Tristan legend by Malory, Wagner, and Bédier, which are the only ones Joyce is known specifically to refer to. The closest thing to the cave in these is Joyous Gard, a splendidly furnished castle that Launcelot lends to Malory's Trystram and Isode. While there, they indulge their sexuality completely: "they made joy togydrys [together] dayly with all maner of myrtthis that they coude devyse" (506). In the Games chapter this site of *jouissance* appears as a tone of youthful hope in Anna's voice linked to gender reform (and orgasm). Actually, it is what she hears the bubbles saying in the pot she stirs, but a person who hears enthusiastic words coming from popping bubbles is projecting and virtually singing sotto voce:

the coming man, the future woman, the food that is to build, what he with fifteen years will do, the ring in her mouth of joyous guard, stars astir and stirabout. (*FW* 246.11–14)

A woman who makes food for her children is working for the future, and so women are oriented toward reform. ALP sees one of her sons as a new kind of man and sees her daughter as a heroine singing a song of freedom—so Joyous Gard ends up in Issy's mouth. As I have suggested, Issy is Anna's song of the future, so their voices mix. Anna goes on dreaming of what her children will achieve, and then worrying about how Issy will manage the choice between the two brothers. She must hope "the future woman" will free herself, for now a version of the key line of the Song of Deborah appears: "And lead raptivity captive" (FW 246.19).[5] The main change in this line is the first letter of "raptivity," which indicates that Anna does not want her daughter to be raped as she was. Rather Issy, by being cool (she is called "Icy" on the next line), will control her man's inclination to rape by assuming the active role and making him rapt. Like Deborah, but in a new way, she will be working for human progress by civilizing man.

Hayman (56–92) shows that Joyce intended the *Wake* to be at least partly a version of the Tristan legend from 1923 on; and Tim Martin, citing hundreds of references to Wagner's *Tristan und Isolde* in the *Wake* (195–204), says that this work bears the same relation to the *Wake* that the *Odyssey* does to *Ulysses* (97). Therefore, it is hard to believe that Joyce did not know Gottfried's poem, which was Wagner's source and is generally regarded (though it is incomplete) as the greatest version of the tale.

Gottfried's cave in the forest was made by giants, with Gothic trimmings and windows. Here the lovers spend their happiest time, doing whatever they want and living on nothing but love, which is their food (English *Tristan* 261–62). Gottfried also says, "The service they received was the song of birds, of the lovely, slender nightingale, the thrush and blackbird, and other birds of the forest" (English *Tristan* 263). He goes on to show two birds competing to see who can serve the lovers best, a Disney touch.

Every detail of the cave is presented as symbolic of love's virtues, and although it is not called a chapel, it is certainly a temple of love, which Gottfried treats devoutly as a religion (English *Tristan* 42, 44). Denis de Rougemont (133) says that the *Minnegrotte* is a church, with its bed as altar. I think the cave stands for the peaceful and miraculous space lovers make between themselves as a sort of shared womb. It is located far from civilization to signify that it is opposed to ordinary reality. This ideal love cannot last, and the lovers are bound to be tracked down by the establishment (Mark). They could not represent the full intensity of love if they were not tragically doomed.

Minne, the medieval German word for courtly love, is famous in combination with *singer*; and the chapel is linked to music because the

German *die Kapelle* means not only "chapel" but "band" (thus Bach's title of *Kappelmeister*). ALP's rivering voice is described as a "minne-lisp extorreor" (*FW* 254.13), a play on interior monologue that means a burning love lisp. And in the chapter in which the voices of the characters emerge from the sleeping Yawn (Shaun in III.3), Issy's voice links a chapel to *Minne* indirectly when she dreams of her wedding. Two more German words here are *bloss*, "naked," and *Blick*, "look": "It will all take bloss as oranged at St Audiens rosan chocolate chapelry with my diamants blickfeast after at minne owned hos . . ." (*FW* 528.5–7).

Of course making love is the opposite of marriage in this adulterous legend. Much of the power of Gottfried's work derives from his opposition to conventional religious and social values, and I am partial to the unprovable conjecture that Gottfried's *Tristan* is incomplete because he was killed for making a religion of love.[6] While marriage and love are opposed by many continental courtly poets, the struggle to combine them has been central to British literature since Chaucer. Joyce's version recognizes the need for mates to mar each other and to make each other aloof. He insists on the brutality of the gender system in marriage, but also on a core of sharing and giving. The utopian aspect of love is one of the bases of progressive thought, and a working marriage may be the best model for the principle that what is mine is yours. The chapel as a place where gender conflict is abrogated represents the possibility of reaching beyond the active-passive polarity into a free interchange of feeling with the other.

The image of the cave, however, suggests that this center of selflessness has been implanted in women. They have sustained it, while men have partaken of it, have dropped in on it. Gottfried gives the proper title of the cave as *la fossiure a la gent amant*" (English *Tristan* 261, 267), and *la fosse*, which means 'ditch,' suggests the female sex organ. The *Wake* uses this root to refer to ALP's pudendum: "herit fossyending" (*FW* 298.4–5). In fact, the Middle High German word for cave that Gottfried uses when he is not affecting French is *hol* (German *Tristan* II 215–16). In Blake's "I saw a chapel all of gold," the chapel is feminine sexuality corrupted by phallic violation:

> I saw a serpent rise between
> The white pillars of the door
> And he forcd & forcd & forcd
> Down the golden hinges tore.
> (Blake 458)

In II.4, the chapter of the *Wake* that concentrates on Tristan and Isolde, Joyce uses the term *chapel* to refer to a vagina from which a penis withdraws with the onomatopoeic verb *plip*: "that was her knight of the truths thong plipping out of her chapellledeosy, after where he had gone and polped the questioned. Plop" (*FW* 396.31–33). Male dignity gets scant credit here, for the word "Plop" represents both his withdrawal and his proposal from a female point of view as defecation.

The chapel as womb, the unconscious in which people immerse themselves when they make love, corresponds to the conflict-free area that D. W. Winnicott (11–16) says a mother makes for her child so that he can feel free to expand into playful possibilities. Winnicott (118–21) argues that all creative thought requires a recreation of the boundaryless space that the mother provided. The usual male attitude is rigidly defensive, so a man must project himself into maternal space before he can open up to new connections. This is why for thousands of years it was understood that when a man was inspired, an imaginary woman, the muse, would enfold him.

Within this "chapelofeases" (*FW* 571.11), which woman is responsible for providing, repression is lifted so that the logical oppositions of rational thought are abrogated.[7] Moreover, as I suggested, men and women exchange genders in the give-and-take of lovemaking, so that each lover recovers the bisexual state of infancy before gender differentiation represented by another version of chapel, "young Chappielassies" (*FW* 607.15). This phrase also suggests a new generation free of sex divisions. In the space of exchange all terms are shifting and displaced, as suggested by "Qu'appelle?" (*FW* 197.08).

However creative this may be, the term "chapelofeases" shows how the release woman provides is not valued. It is merely a convenience, like the "manzinahurries" (*FW* 214.3), a public bathroom: "chapelofeases, sold for a song" (*FW* 571.11). What happens at the end is that Anna sets out to find the lost chapel of her marriage, but as she moves toward this chapel, she realizes her responsibility for it and makes it her own. As she does so, however, she confronts the impossibility of claiming herself, and to understand this impossibility, we must recognize the power Joyce ascribed to marriage.

THE PROSPECTOR

In Lacanian terms, the space in the chapel is the space of looping interchange with the Other, as represented by the opposite sex, and it is only through such contact with the Other that one can know oneself. A stable relationship allows continuous interaction that reaches toward another person, through whom one can fully see oneself, whereas in temporary relations, one is less likely to see beyond one's own fantasies, and this is an important reason for Joyce's support of marriage.

This is not marriage as contract, and in fact Richard Brown (40) has shown that ALP and HCE, who have different surnames, are probably not formally married, as Joyce and Nora were not for most of their years together. What Joyce means by marriage is a deep interchange of identities and genders, the projecting of one's life and future on another person. Joyce invokes this bond as ALP and HCE prepare to make love in the chapter in which they are seen in bed (III.4):

> Prospector projector and boomooster giant builder of all causeways woesoever, . . . zeal whence to goal whither, wonderlust, in sequence to which every muckle must make its mickle, . . . being the only wise in a muck's world to look on itself from beforehand; mirrorminded curiositease and would-to-the-large which bring hills to molehunter, home through first husband, perils behind swine and horsepower down to hungerford, prick this man and tittup this woman, our forced payrents. . . . (FW 576.18–27)

This invocation to copulation is a parody of Milton's invocation to the combination of marriage and love in Book IV of *Paradise Lost*, as Adam and Eve copulate:

> Hail wedded Love, mysterious Law, true source
> Of human offspring, sole propriety
> In Paradise of all things common else.
> By thee adulterous lust was driv'n from men
> Among the bestial herds to range, by thee
> Founded in Reason, Loyal, Just, and Pure,
> Relations dear, and all the Charities
> Of Father, Son, and Brother first were known.
> (lines 750–57)

Parallels confirm the source: both passages hail love, claim exclusive powers for it, and list the range of its accomplishments. Both are heard as a couple who represent marriage, though they are not formally married, are making love. And Joyce even refers to HCE and ALP as Adam and Eve, for "our forced payrents" is "our first parents."

Naturally, Joyce thoroughly reverses Milton's values, for Milton has a harsh attitude toward women; and through his allegiance to Cromwell, he is an enemy of Ireland. For Milton, love is a patriarchal "Law" founded on reason and focused on "propriety" and legitimacy. His first two lines imply that the illegitimate are not human, which would include Joyce's children. Milton separates people who are acceptable, "Father, Son, and Brother," from those who have "lust," but Joyce celebrates desire, "wonderlust," as the only force that can take one out of oneself and as the source of all motivation. What is most valuable about desire for Joyce is that it breaks down propriety, creating categories rather than fitting into them. Once desire displaces one, some sort of creation, though it may be squandered, is inevitable: "every muckle must make its mickle [much]."

McHugh notes a reference to a row of ancient stones in Antrim called the Giant's Causeway in "giant builder of all causeways woesoever." This says that desire, as wanderlust, can go anywhere and build anything, though it implies that the goal will inevitably turn out to be woe. Desire can change topography by bringing "hills to molehunter," a combination of bringing the mountain to Mohammed and making it out of a molehill. On the sexual level, this means that desire can make small protuberances feel like big ones. The general feeling is that anything can be transformed.

The sexual level of the passage can be gross. "Perils behind swine," for example, means that a person who feels enough desire will not let any threat stop him, but it does call him a swine. "Boomooster" combines a series of phallic terms, including "boom," "rooster," "bullmoose," and "booster." "Would-to-the-large" suggests erection, but it also suggests imaginative expansion, largess. The emphasis on the imaginary represents the phallus as an illusion, and ALP shares it through her stiff nipples.

Whereas Milton presents a world where everything is shared, but love is property, Joyce celebrates love as the only way to go beyond selfish enclosures. The central power of the wonder of lust here is that only desire allows one to see the other end of the circuit that constitutes one. It leads to the interchange with the Other which is the only means of development. In this sense, the "mirrorminded curiositease" of desire breaks up and disintegrates the self, so it can have its terrifying aspect.

6

The Terror and Pity of Love
ALP's Soliloquy

The greater the love, the more false its object.

—W. H. Auden

THE ENGENDERED SUBJECT AND THE CYCLE OF SIGNIFICATION

If, as Lacan says, what psychoanalysis "discovers in the unconscious is the whole structure of language" (*Écrits* 147), then the structure of language is repressed. For Lacan, the self is built on a language structure of division, but this division must be held under to maintain the illusion of a unified identity. Terror inheres in this conflict because the self cannot survive without the divided structure of desire that destroys it, de-sires it. For the other, disintegrative side of language operates in a submerged field behind desire and love.

The major linguistic system in this field opposed to consciousness is the cultural construct known as woman. She is designed to contain the interplay between self and Other, and so she is outside the definable signs of the Symbolic order. Irigaray puts it strongly, "Women don't have a soul: they serve as guarantee for man's" (97). They make his subjectivity possible by living the division he projects on them. Joyce's powerful analysis of this construct in ALP's soliloquy at the end of the *Wake* confronts the divided aspect of language that constitutes and undermines the subject through desire.

For Lacan, the desire to signify is the determinant of sexual desire and forms the subject. As a signifier, the subject strives to maintain its unity and definition; but it is divided because a signifier has meaning only in relation to other signifiers. The phallus, as the power to signify, is linked by culture to masculinity, while woman is constructed so that,

81

to quote Lacan, she "finds the signifier of her own desire in the body of the one to whom she addresses her demand for love" (*FS* 84). He is culturally situated as the sign of her unity and authority.

Lacan holds that the subject as signifier consists of a cycle of interchange between the self and an unknowable Other, but this cycle is concealed, and a major means of concealing it is gender. The masculine structure pushes its signifier forward to impose it on the feminine, while the feminine is designed to receive it from the male. In this culturally shaped imbalance, each maintains "shis" gender by avoiding the realization that (s)he is an interchange with the other. The man generally displaces his interchange onto the woman, while she displaces her unity onto him. To be a man, he has to forget the extent to which, starting with mother, he is defined by woman; but to be a woman, she must forget the extent to which she defines man.

The tragic dimension of love rests on this division, that one cannot sustain a knowledge of the loop that creates one through the other. Such division is implied by Stephen's definition of the tragic emotion in *Portrait* as "a face looking two ways, towards terror and towards pity, both of which are phases of it" (*P* 178–79). This emotion cannot exist without being divided, and pity and terror are defined so as to correspond to self and other; for while both phases arrest "the mind in the presence of whatsoever is grave and constant in human suffering," pity "unites" the mind with "the human sufferer," while terror unites it with "the secret cause" (*P* 178). We pity the tragic hero(ine) because (s)he turns against shis own self-interest, and (s)he terrifies us because (s)he turns toward a principle beyond life. These two sides correspond to Lacan's theory of the tragic heroine as between two deaths—physical death and symbolic death—which I will use to describe ALP's final phase.

The tragic division between self and other in love is ordered by the cultural polarization of people into male and female constructs. Joyce's men, insofar as they are intelligent, recognize that they cannot fulfill the male role of autonomous signifier. This is the realization that Stephen attributes to Shakespeare in "Scylla and Charybdis," and it is shared by Stephen and Bloom. The men in Joyce's work who ignore the power of women to define them and believe that they fill the male role, such as Blazes Boylan, are virtually unconscious. And women in Joyce are conscious to the extent that they recognize that the authority of the men to whom they are subject is a projection of their own minds. For both genders, then, intelligence consists of recognizing the cycle. But the genderation of Joyce's women makes them return to the belief that their consciousness is centered by a man, just as the men are addicted to their masculinity.

ALP, enclosed by the feminine structure, keeps trying to center her identity on an absolute male standard that keeps failing. She projects the phallus as the secret cause that makes her suffer a constant sense of loss. But there is an element in her that sees through this delusion, and it comes to the fore at the end of the book. With this realization, she casts off the gender system and approaches pure alterity. Casting off the system has destructive effects she can barely handle, but she has to move through this destruction to sustain the truth that moves the work in its progress. At the end, the *Wake* focuses on the aspect of her mind that turns against male authority in its search for the lost chapel of Izod, her own being as a woman. In doing so, she enters a tragic zone beyond ordinary life, so that it becomes useful to describe her situation in terms of Lacan's analysis of *Antigone*.

ALP's letter, which precedes and in effect prefaces her soliloquy, is introduced as the return of the veritable self. Throughout the *Wake* it has been anticipated as the document that contains the truth, a microcosm of the *Wake* world. Now its longest form follows directly on the description of the "vicociclometer" that passes life through a cycle of "decomposition" and "recombination"—as in sleep, digestion, or sex—to return all "the *h*eroticisms, *c*atastrophes and *e*ccentricities transmitted by the *a*ncient *l*egacy of the *p*ast" (*FW* 614.35–615.1, my italics).

ALP's role in producing HCE and history (Herodotus) is indicated by a series of references to the washerwomen: "all your horodities will incessantlament be coming back from the Annone Wishwashwhose . . . every article lathering leaving several rinsings so as each rinse results with a dapperent rolle . . ." (*FW* 614.1–6). Like most artists, she composes out of her suffering, and her incessant laments sustain his oddities and her own. "The sameold gamebold adomic structure" of gender will be back if she lets it "as sure as herself pits hen to paper and there's scribings scrawled on eggs" (*FW* 615.6–10). The human identity she will write at the waking that will make the dream world die is here shown to include genetic continuity, which exists only through the intercourse between men and women. Now the letter appears directly after the line "Of cause, so! And in effect, as?" (*FW* 615.11), indicating that this is it, the structure of human consciousness. It consists of a woman's discourse because man derives his being from her thought, but the woman's voice in the letter is primarily concerned with defending her man because she derives her identity from his. If, as Lacan holds, identity comes into existence with gender, then both male and female identities depend on her believing in him, a faith that must be stronger for its impossibility. But behind her conventional role in the letter is a flood of resentment and desire that follows it.

Lacan seems to say that woman and man are symptoms of each other in one of his talks on Joyce, "Joyce the Symptom II," for he first says that "a woman . . . is the symptom of another body" and then adds, "Even though paradoxically only another symptom interests her."[1] This other symptom may be man as her symptom, for he embodies an ideal of unity and autonomy that she desires. The constant striving of men to be men is performed directly or indirectly for women (mates or mothers), even when it is distorted into violence or cruelty. Irigaray's response to the idea that the genders are symptoms of each other might be that we should not rule out the possibility that these symptoms can be cured, and this visionary possibility has a place in the *Wake*'s finale.

Related to the idea of man and woman as symptoms of each other is the question of to whom the letter is addressed. It appears to be addressed to a man in authority, a higher level of HCE. The letter opens, "Dear. And we go on to Dirtdump. Reverend. May we add majesty?" (*FW* 615.12–13). Hart (200) points out that "Reverend" sounds like "riverrun," the first word of the *Wake*. It also sounds like river end and the end of the dream (French *rêve*), corresponding to the oceanic father who arises at the book's end, and who is linked to HCE.

Yet the letter speaks of HCE in the third person more often than the second, so it may not be fully addressed to him. Patrick McCarthy (97–100) calls the addressee into question by pointing out that there are many versions of the letter throughout the *Wake*, and there is no way to be sure that any one is more authoritative than any other. Though the last one seems to be the most complete, it leaves out many elements in earlier ones. McCarthy notes that the version of the letter that appears in the Letter chapter (I.5) is addressed to "Maggy" (*FW* 111.10), and that the interpretation of the letter in this chapter derives "your majesty" from "Maggy's tea" (*FW* 116.24). Therefore the letter may be addressed to Issy's mirror friend as well as to HCE. Considering the multiplicity of language in any letter, Derrida speaks in *The Post Card* of "the impossibility that a unique addressee ever be identified" (81). Every letter is addressed to more than one person.

Just as men often pick women to impress other actual or imaginary men, the love a woman has for a man will tend to be partly addressed to other women. The gossipy tone of the letter sometimes sounds as if it is between women: "How delitious for the three Sulvans of Dulkey and what a sellpriceget the two Peris of Monacheena!" (*FW* 616.10–12); "Well, we simply like their demb cheeks, the Rathgarries, wagging here about around the rhythms in me amphybed . . ." (*FW* 619.6–7). So it may be that ALP's defense of HCE is addressed to women as well as to him; and it must continue to be addressed to women when it slips from defense into criticism and dismissal.

HER OTHER HE

Yet much of ALP's mind strives to keep down such criticism and such division of identity. As HCE's supporter she wants him to stand clear or stand out clearly as a unity. In her letter and soliloquy, she repeatedly calls on him to "Rise up. . . . And stand up tall! Straight" (*FW* 619.25, 620.1). "Her untitled mamafesta memorialising the Mosthighest" (*FW* 104.4) aims to elevate him in every way. For example, at the start of the following passage, she has faith that his first thoughts were noble:

the best of our belief in the earliest wish of the one in mind was the mitigation of the king's evils. And how he staired up the step after it's the power of the gait. His giantstand of manunknown. No brad wishy washy wathy wanted neither! Once you are balladproof you are unperceable. . . . (*FW* 616.28–32)

She calls him "the one" because she wants to believe that there has always been this single figure in her mind, even in childhood. As a child he wanted to help the king or cure with the royal touch (which McHugh tells us was supposed to cure "the king's evil," scrofula). HCE's vigorous stride up the stairway showed his strength, and to him is attributed Wellington's megaphallic monument or the sentimental associations of the Tomb of the Unknown Soldier or the power of the Welsh seagod Mananaan. His must be a giantstand, not merely a brad, a small, thin nail.

Yet ALP's asseverations about HCE subvert themselves, like most of the discourse of the *Wake*. The syntax of the first sentence indicates that her belief in his good intentions mitigates *his* evils—but behind her idealization, a debased reality is suggested. He stared up the stairs at her as they walked, as Gabriel Conroy stares at Gretta in "The Dead," with a good view of her moving buttocks: "She mounted the stairs . . . her skirt girt tightly about her. He could have flung his arms about her hips . . ." (*D* 215). ALP grants that she would like "to drag attentions to our Wolkmans Cumsensation Act. The magnets of our midst"

(*FW* 616.24–26). She uses the magnetism of her middle to perform a sensational act that compensates workmen (or dreamers, for *Wolk* means "cloud" in German). The power of her gait evidently gave him come sensations, for he seems to have been nursing an erection, and this "giantstand of manunknown" may have been promoted by his not being seen. The passage has a sordid underside: after all, it is clear why she insists (in a reference to "The Ballad of Persse O'Reilly," *FW* 44–47) that he is balladproof and unpierceable—because he is not. In fact, he is impossible.

ALP is anxious to separate HCE from his negative side, which she represents as his enemy Magrath. McHugh in his *Sigla* (126–32) identifies Magrath as one of the main people behind the slanderous ballad and a competitor of HCE's in the grocery business, though HCE is mainly an innkeeper. ALP accuses Magrath of corruption, which means mixing identities. HCE "never put a dramn in the swags but milk from a national cowse," whereas one of Magrath's crimes is the corruption of butter by mixing it with bacon grease:[2] "bacon what harmed butter! It's margarseen oil. Thinthin thinthin" (*FW* 615.26–32). This loss of unity echoes the original sin at the "Magazine Wall" (*FW* 45.4). Though the Magazine Wall is a place in Phoenix Park, this sin may have corrupted reality by involving sex with a magazine. It is original in the sense that many modern adolescents have their first sex with "maggies." In any case, this sin was performed by HCE, not Magrath.

At this point, ALP, as McHugh points out, proclaims a combination of the eighth, ninth, and tenth commandments: "Stringstly is it forbidden by the honorary tenth commendmant to shall not bear full sweetness against a nighboor's wiles" (*FW* 615.32–33). Here again her words subvert themselves, for the double negative of this "commendmant" requires adultery. Yet compromised as it may be, her decalogic injunction against adultery and adulterating insists on unity; whereas Magrath is represented by his henchman, Sully, whose name refers to mixing through staining or soiling.

She says that she could get HCE's enemy destroyed "in contravention to the constancy of chemical combinations not enough of all the slatters of him left for Peeter the Picker to make their threi sevelty filfths of a man out of" (*FW* 616.7–10). The man being attacked here, Magrath, is not easily distinguished from the one he traduces, "A nought in nought Erinishmhan, called Ervigsen by his first mate. May all similar douters of our oldhame story have that fancied widming!" (*FW* 616.2–4).

Perhaps the simplest reading of this is that all local daughters should have husbands as good as HCE, but there is a lot more going on. The word *dout* means "put out or extinguish," and "douters" should refer to Magrath as the devilish doubter; but it seems grammatically to refer to HCE, the "Ervigsen" of the previous sentence, and he is rendered suspicious by The Letter's replacing of "out and out" with "nought in nought." If "widming" refers to wedding, then of the male doubters, HCE should have it; but if it means "whipping," it applies to Magrath. As "fancy women," it should go to HCE, but for Magrath, they should only be fancied. The language mixes both men thoroughly.

It is easy to break down Magrath's "chemical combinations" because he lacks the real unity of a compound. In contrast she insists that HCE has always ("from a child") been "of highest valency for our privileged beholdings *e*ver *c*omplete *h*airy of *c*hest, *h*amps and *e*yebags" (*FW* 616.13–14, my italics). Valency is the combinative power of an element, so she asserts his unity for her exclusive seeing and holding. The double iteration of HCE as ECH and CHE in these lines is an effort to insist on his name, yet his name takes a different form every time it appears.

Late in her letter ALP says she will have Magrath "broken into potters pance which would be the change of his life" (*FW* 618.32–33). The change of his life represents the end of his sexual power, as he is reduced to small change or clay pennies. Compare the scene in Zora Neale Hurston's *Their Eyes Were Watching God* (1937) in which the protagonist, Janie Crawford, destroys her domineering husband Joe Starks by announcing in public that when his pants go down, he looks like "de change uh life" (75). After this, Joe is ashamed in front of everyone, turns out to be ill, and soon dies. Anyone articulated as a man needs his manhood to survive. ALP says she would "let out" what would "make a carpus of somebody" (*FW* 616.5–6). Virtually every woman knows a secret that would destroy her man if it were made public, and the closer the couple, the worse the secret tends to be. Whatever the peculiarity of any particular man, the secret is always that the phallus is an illusion.

ALP's efforts to eliminate the enemy are futile for several reasons. As we've noticed, she is constantly confusing the foe with HCE. When she disparages "that coerogenal hun" (*FW* 616.20), for example, it seems to be meant for Magrath, but it includes CEH and sounds like her co-erotic mate. Her efforts to isolate the authentic HCE are shadowed by Magrath, so any attempt to address her beloved will be displaced by alternatives: "Well, here's lettering you erronymously anent other clerical fands allieged herewith. I wisht I wast be that dumb tyke and he'd wish it was me yonther heel" (*FW* 617.30–32). The first meaning for *anent* in the OED is "in line or company with," and "fands" includes (among other things) "friends," "fans," and "fiends." Since the second sentence is clearly about Magrath, it is evident that both sentences add up to say that she cannot address HCE without also writing to Magrath, among others. HCE can only be a multiplicity because the subject is always divided. In the previous chapter, as they are copulating, ALP stimulates HCE by invoking Magrath: "Tipatonguing him on in her pigeony linguish . . . to scorch her faster, faster. . . . Magrath he's my pegger, he is . . ." (*FW* 584.3–6).

If any attempt to reach HCE always aims at a series of possibilities, it is also true that she is divided: "The magnets of our midst being foisted upon by a plethorace of parachutes" (*FW* 616.25–26). Her central gap is surrounded by a crowd of alternative chutes vying to replace it. These include other women and other orifices of hers that compete for his desire. Such para-chutes ease his fall or hold him up.

Even if the enemy who shadows ALP's marriage is a different man from her husband, he is inseparable from their love as the third party involved in passion. René Girard (9–12) argues that desire cannot exist without a rival to act as mediator because the presence of opposition defines what is desirable. This is one way in which HCE could not exist in ALP's life without Magrath. But she is obsessed with separating the two parts of this complex in order to assert HCE's purity, his autonomy, by shifting his division onto his enemy.

The letter concludes by insisting that HCE is not the negative side denied, but the positive side promoted:

Hence we've lived in two worlds. He is another he what stays under the himp of holth. The herewaker of our hamefame is his real namesame who will get himself up and erect, confident and heroic when but, young as of old, . . . a wee one woos. (*FW* 619.11–15)

The HCE who is dead is another one, she asserts; but as for the one who she insists is real, present, and the same as his name, she can only claim he will appear. He continues to be "now about to get up" (*FW* 616.1–2). She implies and conceals the realization that he is dead. And she blames herself, for "get himself up . . . when but, young" implies that if she could be younger, he would wake.

ALP's postscript may parallel the conclusion of the letter by presenting a woman who is both alive and dead. This woman expresses two voices in ALP. One is most like Issy, but Issy as she matures is replacing

ALP, a replacement that is congruent with ALP's death. That is, the lifelong process of Issy's maturation and the lifelong decline of her mother will tend, with some interruption from other factors, to be always in step. Now the phase of youth maturing, the voice of Issy, is heard in her mother: "And she's about fetted up now with nonsery reams. And rigs out in regal rooms with the ritzies" (FW 619.17–18). This shows her flourishing with a blasé glamour. But on another level that could be called deep below, the youth that ALP feels causes a reacting sense of decline.

Therefore ALP's voice is also heard in Issy's, for the daughter, whose glamour has had an ironic undertone all along, turns to making fun of herself. Now she remembers the process of her mother's death, which expresses a lower level of both of their minds, the moribund part: "Rags! Worns out. But she's still her deckhuman amber too" (FW 619.19). ALP's second version, document number two, is laid out in amber, buried in the earth as one level of HCE is. Her ambivalence about him is ambivalence about herself, and the dead part of him she denies is part of her. Whether Issy is a voice in ALP or ALP is a voice in Issy depends on how the series of containing voices is framed.

ALP's discourse goes beyond the ending of the letter to constitute a soliloquy that expresses feelings outside the letter's defensive formality. This is what Lacan speaks of as the *jouissance* of the woman "which goes beyond" (FS 147). In fact, the galley proofs for this part of the *Wake* originally had the end of the letter followed by "Ps" followed by the soliloquy (*JJA* 63.317). The soliloquy was then crossed off this page, and an early version of the final P.S. was added by hand (*JJA* 63.316). Perhaps Joyce originally intended the monologue to be a postscript, but then decided to add one in the ironic style of the letter. This confirms that the soliloquy is a continuation on a lyrical level of what is implied in the letter, of feelings the letter holds under.

The soliloquy continues to express ambiguity about whether HCE is alive: "Rise up, man of the hooths, you have slept so long! Or is it only so mesleems?" (FW 619.25–26). Here the man she calls to is the one buried in the Hill of Howth (pronounced "hooth"), though she said at the end of the letter that the one "under the himp of holth" (FW 619.12) was not the one who would rise, but another. Her exclamation at the extraordinary length of his sleep has eerie overtones. She also has an intuition, when she wonders if it is "only so mesleems," that somehow her perception is responsible for his death. Moreover, linking woman's view to the other world, she fears that her recognition of his death is "only Muslim" or impious illusion.

Joyce presents her love for HCE so as to indicate something destructive in the way love has to be expressed in language. For example, she is overflowing with love when she urges him to stand up tall (*FW* 620.1) and come do what they always wanted to do (*FW* 620.10). And here her enthusiasm leads her to see a series of men in him: "You make me think of a wonderdecker I once. Or somebalt that sailder, the man megallant, with the bangled ears. Or an earl was he, at Lucan? Or, no, it's the Iren duke's I mean. Or somebrey erse from the Dark Countries" (*FW* 620.6–10). These lines—which are followed by "Come and let us!"—indicate strong erotic attraction. The intense focus on HCE's image compels her to see five other men—and each is less clear than the one before. She is moving toward otherness, "somebrey erse," which may be what ultimately attracts her. The multiplicity of truth is reflected by her shifting through the four gospellers to the grey ass that follows them in the *Wake*.

ALP's series of romantic figures misrepresents HCE radically: seeing him as a series of other men, she does not see him as himself. Whenever one describes or perceives an object, one can only use signs whose origin is alien to that object; so the inability of one lover to know another parallels the inability of the signifier to connect with the signified. Moreover, the discourse of romance makes her project him as a series of swashbucklers, a phallic ideal no man could actually live up to in the long run.

Therefore when ALP calls HCE, she is calling someone else, someone nonexistent. She wants to give HCE life by her love, but her love is not directed at him, for it is built into the semiotic system of love to be misdirected. The other to whom one relates is finally not any particular other, but the unknowable otherness or Other behind language that desire aims at. This misdirection is shadowed by fatality, because if desire comes from the Other and the self is formed by reflection, then there is no life or psychic existence that does not come from the love of another person. So in diverging from HCE, ALP inflicts the fatality indicated by the line from Hamlet (3.2.190) cited twice in *Ulysses*: "None wed the second but who killed the first."[3] She feels she will cause his death if she does not stay in touch with him.

Of course, man is not oriented toward bearing such responsibility for the psychic life of woman, and HCE shows little concern for ALP's personal individuality. Chodorow (74) says men are more emotionally dependent on women than women are on them because women tend to be nurturing while men tend to be self-assertive. ALP is caught in the semiotic bind of relationship because she is driven by the need to strive to sustain HCE.

BESIDE THE CORPSE

In her effort to make contact with him, ALP takes HCE's hand, urging him to give it as if he had been holding it back. But the figures she addresses are King Arthur and a bear: "Fy arthou! Come! Give me your great bearspaw, padder avilky . . ." (FW 621.20–21). Since *ilke* is Middle English for "each, every," HCE is here seen as "the limp father of thousands" (U 5.571). As a bear, he is a totem animal, and therefore, like Arthur (whose name means bear) he is dead, unless we believe in him. The description of his hand, however, as Henke (198) observes, soon turns phallic: "Reach down. A lil mo. So. Draw back your glave. Hot and hairy, hugon, is your hand! Here's where the falskin begins. Smoos as an infams" (FW 621.24–26). The word "glave" combines *glove* with Middle English *glaive*, "spear or sword," which suggests the male organ, as does "hot and hairy." Describing this organ, she draws back the foreskin, which is wrinkled, to see the head, which is smooth. This indicates to her that he has a baby-pure inner core even though his exterior, which is what she actually sees, has been damaged in many ways, including chemical corruption, apparently through photography, but generally as a result of experience:

One time you told you'd been burnt in ice. And one time it was chemicalled after you taking a lifeness. Maybe that's why you hold your hodd as if. And people thinks you missed the scaffold. Of fell design. I'll close my eyes. So not to see. Or see only a youth in his florizel, a boy in innocence, peeling a twig, a child beside a weenywhite steed. The child we all love to place our hope in for ever. All men has done something. Be the time they've come to the weight of old fletch. We'll lave it. (FW 621.26–33)

One implication of his being "chemicalled" is that he is called mixed, for Skeat identifies the Greek root behind *chem* as meaning "mix." I find no reference to the main photographer in the *Wake*, Lewis Carroll, as having been injured by chemicals, though he preferred the messy wet plate photography to the simpler dry plate (F. B. Lennon 165). Joyce probably intends the corruption of the phallus by photography to refer to the tendency of men to prefer pinup photos to real women, a tendency already evident in Leopold Bloom. "Taking a lifeness" can mean having intercourse with a photo.

As Henke (198) notices, ALP hopes to wash away HCE's corruption, "lave it." She wants to see him as pure and smooth as an infant, a peeled twig, a little white steed—a series of images of the phallus not as a penis, but as a magic wand. Here is a common pattern among old married couples: what they see may be blighted by age, but they have a magic for each other because they remind each other of earlier images. As usual, however, the sentiment has a disturbing side: the good little boy ALP projects is *her* phallus, and by turning to it, she betrays HCE.[4]

What ALP sees is covered with the false skin of scars and has been severely injured by life; in fact, HCE seems to have been killed. The statement that he "missed the scaffold. Of fell design" implies that as hod carrier he fell off his scaffold intentionally, committing suicide. Also prominent is the idea that he was hung: by cruel design, his feet were deprived of the floor of the scaffold. Late in the Tavern chapter (II.3), HCE was hanged in some detail: "He's doorknobs dead! And Annie Delap is free!" (*FW* 377.36–378.2). That he now holds his "hodd as if" implies not only that he cannot get an erection, but that his head is bent to the side because his neck is broken. Irishmen, through colonial oppression, were traditionally shadowed by the threat of hanging.[5]

The image of the dead man predominates over more active images of HCE in this and other sections. And the situation of the woman lying beside a dead man represents the underlying reality of the phallus, which is based on emptiness because it is first and always constituted as a reaction against castration anxiety, as Lacan explains:

Indeed, why not acknowledge that if there is no virility which castration does not consecrate, then for the woman it is a castrated lover or a dead man (or even both at the same time) who hides behind the veil where he calls on her adoration. . . . From then on, it is through this ideal incubus that a receptivity of embrace has to be transposed into the sensitivity of holding the penis. (*FS* 95)

The ideal incubus that she creates to allow her receptivity to generate his phallus is the magic wand she imagines when she closes her eyes "so not to see." The feeling in the *Wake* that everything happens over and over, linked to the sense that part IV represents every morning, suggests that the woman is always holding the man's phallus, whether or not they are together: she has to do what she can constantly to encourage him. The fear that drives her is based on an actuality: without her he would undergo Symbolic death. In "ALP" one of the things

Anna calls to HCE is *"Hello, ducky, please don't die!"* (FW 200.7). This anxiety holds her in thrall to his phallus.

Kathy Acker expresses this aspect of woman's situation strongly in *Blood and Guts in High School.* Her protagonist, Janey, says that Jean Genet underestimates how difficult it is to be a woman:

He thinks all he has to do to be a woman is slobber. He has to do more. He has to get down on his knees and crawl mentally every minute of the day. If he wants a lover, if he doesn't want to be alone every single goddamn minute of the day . . . , he has to perfectly read his lover's mind, silently, unobtrusively, like a corpse, and figure out at every changing second what his lover wants. He can't be a slave. Women aren't just slaves. They are whatever their men want them to be. They are made, created by men. They are nothing without men. (130)

A man may be in thrall to a woman, but rarely will he shape his mind to hers as a woman does with a man. Joyce encountered a milder version of this idea in Mill (15), who says that men claim not only women's obedience, but their sentiments, so that men have a stronger grip on women than the master has on the slave. For Acker, women are less than slaves because they take their whole subjectivity from men; and Anna, at this point, sees all of her satisfaction in the ideal phallus, "The child we all love to place our hope in for ever." In portraying this situation, Joyce reveals its delusory nature, which Anna herself notices as her pages proceed.

ALP invites her incubus to stand up and walk with her, and insofar as she can draw him forth by this invitation, she can save him and give him life. On the following page she imagines him walking with her: "Not such big strides, huddy foddy! You'll crush me antilopes I saved so long for. They're Penisole's. And the two goodiest shoeshoes" (FW 622.8–9). McHugh mentions that "huddy foddy" suggests "holy father," and ALP returns to such an image on her last page. But it is doubtful that HCE is really walking here. To some extent, at least, her vision of him astride is a tragic delusion, like Ophelia's when she sings that she is going to her lover, or Lear's when he imagines at the end that Cordelia speaks.

Vincent J. Cheng (191–92) points out in *Shakespeare and Joyce* that ALP's monologue contains many echoes of Shakespeare's tragic heroines, including Juliet, Ophelia, Desdemona, and Lady Macbeth; but her strongest connections here are with Cleopatra, whom her phrases evoke some five times. Glasheen lists many appearances of Cleopatra in the *Wake*, and they generally represent ALP. Because Cleopatra was a queen of Egypt, this is another way in which Joyce makes Anna African. In fact, Cleopatra was descended from a Macedonian dynasty installed by Alexander the Great, but Shakespeare's Cleopatra, the main one in the *Wake*, refers to herself as "black" (1.5.28).

Barbara Brivic notices another Europeanized African tragic heroine who contributes to Anna's final words. When ALP says "mememormee!" at the end (*FW* 628.14), this is a positive version (Leo Knuth reads it as "me me more me") of the poignant lament that Henry Purcell's Dido repeats at the end of *Dido and Aeneas* (1689), "Remember me." In 1919 Joyce attempted to get this great opera produced in Zurich (*JJ* 454). Purcell's version of the story, based on Nahum Tate's, differs from Virgil's in the *Aeneid*, which justifies the destruction of Carthage by having Dido curse Aeneas as he deserts her at the end of book 4. At this point, however, Virgil's Dido dies in the arms of her sister Anna, who climbs onto the funeral pyre to join her, a great act of sisterhood. This Dido is a woman who stands for Africa as an area that must be conquered if Rome is to thrive, so it is not surprising that Joyce gives preference to Purcell's more compassionate portrayal. Dido appears three lines above "mememormee!" in "die down," but she is a minor figure in the *Wake* compared to Cleopatra.

A cluster of Cleopatra references appears as ALP plays with the Irish phrase that opens her monologue, "Soft morning" (*FW* 619.20), which means "it is drizzling." The late lines "Softly so" (*FW* 624.21), "so soft this morning, ours" (*FW* 628.8), and "Bussoftlhee" (*FW* 628.14, just before the Dido echo) are seen by Cheng as paralleling Cleopatra's reaction to the asp that she allows to bite her to death. Most of her last lines seem to be addressed to her servant Charmian:

> *Cleo.*   Peace, peace!
> Dost thou not see my baby at my breast,
> That sucks the nurse asleep?
>
> *Char.*   O, break! O, break!
> *Cleo.*   As sweet as balm, as soft as air, as gentle—
> O Antony!—Nay, I will take thee too:
>   [*Applying another asp to her arm.*]
> What should I stay—   *Dies.*
>   (5.2.308–11)

In relation to the Cleopatra reference, ALP's "Soft morning" is death, though the earlier scene of the washers playing "Die eve" indicated the inseparability of death, passion, and revolution. Every waking is the death of a dream and the birth of a new one in the *Wake*, and Cleopatra would not be so eager to go if she had no one to go to. Most critics agree that "Nay, I will take thee too" refers to a second asp that she takes to bite her. So the above stage directions appear in almost all editions, though the Folio (the original text) only has "*Dyes.*" It is true that Cleopatra is described at the end as bitten on the breast and arm (5.2.348–50).

Cleopatra, however, does not seem to need another snake when she speaks to "thee," for she dies before completing the next line. I do not think that "Nay, I will take thee too" need be addressed to a second asp. The clown who gives Cleopatra the asp(s) wishes her "joy of the worm" (5.2.260, 279), referring to it repeatedly, as she does (5.2.243), in the singular.

The line "As sweet as balm, as soft as air, as gentle" suggests that the poison has made her delirious. The fact that she is losing consciousness is indicated by the reversal of nursing a baby until it is drowsy: here it "sucks the nurse asleep." Babies sure do bite, but what makes Cleopatra feel a poisonous snake as an infant is love. This is a fine illustration of Lacan's idea of the phallus as an "ideal incubus," so the asp is linked to Antony. Cleopatra gives herself to both of them in death. Earlier she made a witty remark about forgetting something as Antony forgets her: "O, my oblivion is a very Antony" (1.3.90).

I think "O Antony!—Nay, I will take thee too" is addressed to Antony, whom she imagines joining her. Earlier in the scene she saw Antony, who had already killed himself, summoning her to make haste in joining him:

> quick. Methinks I hear
> Antony call; I see him rouse himself
> to praise my noble act . . .
>
>   . . .
>   . . . Husband, I come!
> Now to that name my courage prove my title!
>   (5.2.282–88)

She will marry Antony by suicide, and so they will set out together. The sense that nobility is free because it can choose death, which pervades the end of *Antony and Cleopatra*, may be reflected by ALP, who speaks of her death as voluntary departure. Cleopatra appoints a destination for herself and Antony as she prepares to die: "I am again for Cydnus / To meet Mark Antony" (5.2.228–29). Cydnus is where she first met Antony in her famous barge (2.2.186–218), so she is going back to the scene of her first love. Gretta goes back to her first love at the end of "The Dead," and Molly ends *Ulysses* this way. I believe that ALP does it in the *Wake*, but she goes back to an earlier level of love before HCE and patriarchy. The existence of Cleopatra's goal may help explain "I will take thee too." If Cleopatra does dream of raising Antony and taking him with her—or if Joyce read it this way, as his vision might lead him to—this is the closest parallel for ALP's delusion of raising HCE.

Perhaps I should add, however, that while Frank Kermode calls Cleopatra "the greatest of Shakespeare's female characterizations" (Shakespeare, *Riverside* 1346), *Antony and Cleopatra* is not a feminist play. Cleopatra has many weaknesses, and unlike ALP, she never really questions her devotion to her man. It does occur to her that Antony was a dream of hers, and that this dream was too perfect to be a real man; but she decides to follow the dream rather than reality (5.2.76–100). Joyce saw Shakespeare as conservative, and this was one reason he preferred Ibsen (*JJ* 398). Turning back to ALP, I find emphasis on how the reality of her man conflicts with her dream of him.

Anna stays with the vigorous image of HCE walking for five lines, but then her tone gets elegaic: "It seems so long since, ages since. As if you had been long far away. Afartodays, afeartonights, and me as with you in thadark. You will tell me some time if I can believe its all" (*FW* 622.13–16). He is far away during the days (or "nowadays"), she is afraid at night, and she seems to be with him only in "that" dark. On the level of ALP's parallel to Cleopatra, these lines may be spoken by a woman whose man has passed away, so that she can commune with him only through death. Yet they also speak for many wives with living husbands, men who are always away during the day, cause them to fear at night, and seem to be really with them only in sex.

The universality of such patterns is suggested by their appearance in two Old English lyrics written over a thousand years ago, "The Wife's Lament" and "Wulf and Eadwacer" (Alexander 108–11, 116–17). Both of these present a woman who condemns the man she lives with because he is the enemy of the one she loves, who is absent. Barbara Brivic notes, though it may be coincidental, that Earwicker's name resembles that of Eadwacer, who is usually regarded by interpreters of the obscure poem in which he appears as playing the role of the tyrannical husband. These poems gain power by presenting situations where the missing man is ambiguous and idealized. They suggest an audience of women who could relate to the situation of longing for a man who would be on their side, as opposed to the husbands and kins-men who compelled and possessed them.

ALP's projection into the future of "some time" when HCE will come to tell her if she can really believe in him would fit the pattern of a widow who hopes to join her husband (or God) in heaven, but it also expresses an ongoing insecurity that is common in love, especially the love of women for men. Women are often eager for reassurance be-cause they get so little. Joyce blurs the boundary between having and losing not only for psychological and poetic reasons, but to indicate how unclear that boundary actually is.

The image of HCE and ALP strolling together is rendered pitiful by her feeling that he has been gone for ages, and a few lines further on she says, "I could lead you there and I still by you in bed" (*FW* 622.19–20). These lines suggest that they do not actually get up, a sug-gestion confirmed near the end by "I'll slip away before they're up" (*FW* 627.35). McHugh says in his *Sigla* that at the end of the *Wake* HCE "is still motionless in bed" (106).

I concede that the level on which she walks with him may have as much reality as anything else in this dreamlike text, but most of the time the level of getting up seems to be subordinated to that of staying in bed. Whether they get up or not is indeterminate, and there is beauty in Joyce's conception of a phase of age in which it does not quite matter. But there is also terror in the structure, the secret cause that dictates that whether it is her fault or his, he can never really be there.

THE LOST BODY

Where is ALP taking him, whether or not they get up? She says, "we go out in all directions . . ." (*FW* 618.21), and the goal has many aspects. Irigaray (29) says that when woman tries to express herself, she "sets off in all directions," and self-expression may turn out to be the most comprehensive term for ALP's goal, but then it comprehends quite a bit, including the question of the extent to which she expresses herself through HCE.

The walking imagery suggests sex when ALP asks him to adjust his motion to her own, as Henke (199) points out. The lovemaking of ALP and HCE was referred to as walking in the previous chapter: "Here we shall do a far walk . . ." (*FW* 570.28, and see 567.21). After saying that his "big strides" are crushing her shoes that are "Penisole's," which may suggest that he is rubbing her clitoris too hard, she asks him to move to her rhythm: "A gentle motion all around. *As leisure paces*" (*FW* 622.12–13, my italics). On the other hand, Kim Devlin (*Wandering* 170) suggests that because she says, "Let's our joornee saintomichael make it" (*FW* 621.2), and speaks of going to the "Old Lord" (*FW* 623.4), she may be taking him to his death.

While these levels are involved, ALP speaks more directly and prominently of taking him to a place they often walked to, one that re- calls their youth and romantic feelings for each other. This idea—as well as sex, death, and her self-expression—may be related to her tak- ing him to the field of the Other, Lacan's term for the unknowable oth- erness of the unconscious as something to be approached spatially. If, as Lacan says, each partner in a sexual relation "must stand as the cause of desire" for the other (*FS* 81), then the place ALP can take HCE to in bed is the cause of his desire; and desire, in Lacan, always comes from the Other in the sense that we never know where it comes from. Moreover, Jacqueline Rose points out that "the place of the Other is also the place of God" (*FS* 50), and by including God, the Other in- cludes death. The Other, as Ragland-Sullivan (*Jacques Lacan* 191) ex- plains, is an indefinite remnant of our dependence on our parents, the fact that we were formed by reflection; and as Lemaire (157) indicates, it is also every other word that gives each word meaning. But Irigaray (89, 93) asserts that this Other is a role imposed on woman so that she reflects man at the expense of her own identity and her own body.

HCE may be incomprehensible in himself, but by passing through the field of the Other, he gains the power to signify, as the male organ derives its significance from the female. He gains his unified identity by displacing his otherness onto her. Whatever HCE can express—and indeed his very being is articulated in language—is constituted from his perceptions; and Anna's power centers on creating and defining his perceptions, as she declares: "I'll be your aural eyeness" (*FW* 623.18). By going with her, he can reach the source of sensation and communication.

As the locus of interplay between them, the place she wants to take him to, which is both the scene of love and the palace of the Lord, is the chapel; but her perception of the chapel is changing. One sign of change is that she is leading him. Tristan led Isot to the Cave of Lovers in Gottfried's *Tristan*, reflecting the tendency of men to discover for women the place of exchange that occupied the women's bodies. Anna was subject to these conditions earlier, but now she is in control, telling HCE what to do. She moves in the direction of taking responsibility for the chapel, but at the same time the chapel becomes something lost, something in the distance that is unattainable.

In the Arthurian cycle, the chapel in the distance that is unattainable is the site of the grail. HCE has just appeared as the dying Arthur, and as ALP sets out, she says, "Send Arctur guiddus!" (FW 621.7–8). As Anna struggles toward the impossible goal of her chapel, it comes to correspond to Lacan's term for the lost object of desire that we are always trying to recover, the Thing or *das Ding* (*Ethics* 58). Lacan equates the Thing with the lost body of the mother known in infancy (*Ethics* 67), and Anna's chapel will come to stand on one level for the lost body of womanhood that Irigaray says women knew in the preoedipal stages before they were subject to phallic authority. In the *Wake*, the question of whether this lost body of woman can be sustained apart from man remains in doubt, but the goal of recovering woman's body is taken seriously: it may be no more impossible than the goals of heterosexuality, and it may even serve them.

THE MUTUAL MESSAGE

In an elaborate description of where ALP and HCE will walk to in what seems to be a picnic, she says they will sit "down on the heathery benn [Howth Head], me on you, in quolm unconsciounce. To scand the arising. . . . At the site of salvocean. And watch would the letter you're wanting be coming may be. And cast ashore. That I prays for be mains of me draims" (FW 623.25–31). Margaret Solomon (59–69) points out that the letter in the *Wake* stands for whatever anyone can communicate, especially sexually. In this case, ALP's dreams are prayers, and the man of her dreams will come if the letter arrives, a true communication. This will take place with her on him at the hairy, heated mount ("heathery benn") by her main drain in a place filled with an ocean of salving that is salvation. Here they will not only scan the horizon, but scandalize his erection, and *scandal* derives from the Sanskrit *skand*, "spring up." This intercourse need not be physical: it is the interface where they communicate with themselves through each other. The scene is a jovial assertion of the value of marriage. But through it all she waits for a message that does not arrive, and at the end she is still Brigid praying at her lonely altar (FW 214.2). This is the image of lonely, powerless Irish womanhood that Stephan meditated on in *Portrait* (P 161, 191).

ALP cannot quite define HCE as a signifier, "His giantstand of manunknown" (*FW* 616.30), but she keeps trying to create his identity through her field. We see her shaping him: "Every letter is a hard but yours sure is the hardest crux ever. Hack an axe, hook an oxe, hath an an, heth hith ences" (*FW* 623.33–34). The statement that "Every letter is a hard" links the signifier to the phallus. As ALP strives to carve ("hack"), to weave ("hook"), to hold ("hath") the letter that constitutes him, she slides through four variations that range from primitive axe marks to something that involves hesitancy and metaphysics (for *ens* is Latin for "being"). This letter may be anything at all, and has as much chance of getting through as a message in a bottle. But however misknown it may be, it is given significant form by being received: "But once done, dealt and delivered, tattat, you're on the map" (*FW* 623.35). The medium makes it a message, and ALP's reception makes it signify love./

If ALP produces HCE as a signifier, the lost message is as much hers as his, her message sent onto his land and his message sent into her water: "When the waves give up yours the soil may for me. Sometime then, somewhere there, I wrote me hopes and buried the page when I heard Thy voice, ruddery dunner, so loud that none but, and left it to lie till a kissmiss coming" (*FW* 624.3–6).[6] This passage emphasizes that ALP sends the basis of the message she hopes to receive, yet even her first sending was shaped by the primal male to whom it was addressed. McHugh indicates that "ruddery dunner" includes Roderick O'Connor, the last High King of Ireland, and the German *Donner*, "thunder." Its paternal overtones also include the powers to steer and to dun. The voice of the Father (capitalized as "Thy") shaped her initial message by terminating it, not only inserting her into the Symbolic field of language, but burying the cut-off potential of what she was going to say under that field. Her signification as a woman must now (all her life) wait for its enunciation upon "a kissmiss coming," the arrival and ejaculation while kissing her of a man who combines the Christ child with the Prince who wakes Sleeping Beauty. This is a difficult set of conditions, and as she looks back on them, she sees how delusory they were.

Her message can be articulated only through him, just as his has to be articulated through her. And yet from their wedding night (conventionally optimal), they both found each other swarming with alternate identities. This multiplicity corresponds to lines from the invocation to lust in III.4, which says, "guide them through the labyrinth of their samilikes and the alteregoases of their pseudoselves . . ." (*FW* 576.32–33). Now Anna remembers,

Our native night when you twicetook me for some Marienne Sherry and then your Jermyn cousin who signs hers with exes and the beardwig I found in your Clarksome bag. Pharaops you'll play you're the king of Aeships. (*FW* 624.36–625.4)

McHugh says that "Marienne chérie" is a name for the French Republic, so he took her for French and then for German. But the implication is that he took her *as* French and then as a close cousin (cousin german), one who signed her name with kisses. Husbands may well have moments when they take their wives for or as relatives. Moreover, Joyce had had exotic experiences with French prostitutes before his elopement, so it may be he imagined Nora as French at crucial moments. Unfortunately, one of Nora's main rivals was alcohol, and HCE may have felt the intoxication he derived from ALP as sherry. Other rivals include the Virgin Mary (with her cherry) and Joyce's mother Mary.

As for HCE, his masculine dignity is represented by the false beard or beard-and-wig that he carries in his clerkly or fancy bag,[7] and this "beardwig" may be equated with his identity as Earwigger. If he plays Pharaoh or the King of Asia or of the Fairies (*Aos-sidhe*), or an airplane pilot, she seems to want these roles as much as he does. Women create masculine roles, but neither gender is in control of the system through which they create each other. In this system woman does not know that she has projected what she receives, and man does not know that he has received what he projects. The appearance that man projects and woman receives is therefore unrealistic as well as unfair—but it is in control. While granting its beauty and its power, Joyce is out to dismantle this patriarchal system, or disassemble its cloak, by showing how fundamentally it blights people, especially women.

MEETING AS IMPOSITION

ALP now takes HCE on a tour of the city that seems at times a tour of her body as a series of products. In the lovemaking of the previous chapter, they walked through her landscape in more romantic terms (*FW* 570.27–571.26), but even there her "littleeasechapel" (*FW* 571.18) was a watercloset: "Do your easiness!" (*FW* 571.19). Now she pushes her products harder: "I will tell you all sorts of makeup things, strangerous. And show you every simple storyplace we pass. *Cadmillersfolly, Bellevenue, Wellcrom, Quid Superabit*, villities valleties" (*FW* 625.5–7). She will make up with him by showing him places that are made up, but every feature of her woman's body is constructed by social codes so that her villages and valleys are vile vanities, and they are veiled with language because they can appear only through the system of signs. The language in which woman is written is a kinetic one like advertising, and the first three names in italics are versions of the Gaelic, French, and German for "welcome," as McHugh indicates, while the last means "what shall surpass." She is designed to appeal. And the text now turns back to her childhood to show how she became so commode-ified.

As the tour of the city proceeds, apparently a desperate, isolated version of past tours, ALP notices changes and feels weak. She is almost reduced to tears, and clings to the authority that she projects in HCE. Then she feels the wind pierce her and reaches a crucial point: "Here, weir, reach, island, bridge" (FW 626.7). McHugh notes that the Liffey is tidal to Islandbridge, so this is where the river meets the sea: "Where you meet I" (FW 626.7–8). This implies that the "you" she addresses here has continuously been connected to the father ocean she enters at the end, that husband and father are confused for her.

Such confusion recurs as she goes back to her first meeting with her husband/father: "The day. Remember! Why there that moment and us two only? I was but teen, a tiler's dot" (FW 626.8–9). She was ten or a teen and composed of nothing but misery (teen). She was a tailor's daughter, a tot no bigger than one dot in a mosaic, or only a piece in her culture. HCE appealed to her folly ("fad") because he was like her father ("fad" was "father" in a typescript, JJA 63.262): "The swankysuits was boosting always, sure him, he was like to me fad. But the swaggerest swell off Shackvulle Strutt. And the fiercest freaky ever followed a pining child round the sluppery table with a forkful of fat" (FW 626.9–13).

The bearing of this "sure him" has overtones of child molesting, for the image of the fierce man pursuing ALP with a fork harks back to a passage in the letter in which she denies perverse behavior: "Item, we never were chained to a chair, and, bitem, no widower whother soever followed us about with a fork on Yankskilling Day" (FW 618.24–26). The fork or trident stands for the phallus. Gordon speaks of HCE's tendency to carry a firefork (Plot 22–24, 172). At one point ALP urges him to "Hold up you free fing!" (FW 621.4). This combines three fingers with his phallus and his autonomy. ALP is ostensibly describing her husband as the man with the "forkful of fat," but the image of HCE here seems to be based on a childhood memory, as suggested by the "pining child."

A substantial fraction of girls are molested, and this problem has been underestimated, but what Joyce is concerned with here is not criminal behavior but a larger historical tendency and a universal problem: the unclear border between family affection and incest. A father who never touched his daughter would be wrong, but the child has no way to distinguish what is sexual from what is not. Apparently ALP's father, who is sometimes confused with HCE, followed her around with a forkful of food because she would not eat her meal. In not doing justice to the Thanksgiving feast (which Joyce seems to regard as doing in some Yanks), she was not sufficiently accepting paternal authority. The scene of the fierce figure chasing her around the table, trying to force his fork into her, then became attached in her mind to the image of male aggression, "Captain Finsen . . . pressing for his suit" (FW 624.28–29). On the other hand, the denial of incest here may be seen as a reaction, and the feeding, as a screen. Many women (and some men) will never be sure, and spend their lives ashamed of something they can't quite remember.

As Robert M. Polhemus (78) observes, Joyce himself seems to have been haunted by guilt over his incestuous desire for his disturbed daughter Lucia.[8] There is no evidence that he ever acted on that desire, but her problems would aggravate guilt over wishes. In many ways, the *Wake* is a strong statement about incest. Sandra Gilbert (374–75) levels two charges against Freud on this topic. The first is that he underestimated the prevalence of actual incest as opposed to fantasy, and the second is that he deemphasized the desire of the father to focus on that of the daughter as if she were to blame. In Joyce, however, there is no firm distinction between fantasy and act, so no father is innocent; and Joyce expands enormously on HCE's desire for Issy, showing how it saturates daily life and implying that it is a widespread pattern.

Gilbert cites a quote from Judith Lewis Herman that seems useful here: "overt incest represents only the furthest point in a continuum—an exaggeration of patriarchal family norms, but not a departure from them" (372). Gilbert (371) argues that the daughter is always subject to the father's desire in patriarchal society, and points to Freud's idea that the normal ultimate goal of a woman is to take her father as a lover by giving his authority to her husband. Lacan notices that the incest taboo is primarily against sex between mother and son (*Ethics* 67). The inevitability and "natural" force of patriarchal dominance suffuses all gender relations.

In Joyce's work, the question of whether parents violate children, like the question of whether mates are unfaithful to each other, must always be answered in the affirmative. Joyce's belief that a person can never be unified means that people are bound to impinge on each other and diverge from themselves. From this perspective chastity is a bourgeois ideal. The fact that people must continually violate each other, however, should not be taken to mean that it does not matter if a father seduces his daughter. On the contrary, the realization that parents are bound to violate children makes it all the more necessary to keep that violation to a minimum.

The code that defines masculine and feminine roles causes the man to be constantly pressing on the female, and this usual situation of everyday life is seen in the next lines of the *Wake*: "But a king of whistlers. Scieoula! When he'd prop me atlas against his goose and light our two candles for our singers duohs on the sewingmachine" (*FW* 626.13–15). "Scieoula," which follows her recollecting how attractive he could be, is puzzling. It includes *science, sigh,* and *oo la la,* so it may suggest that the authority of male scientism stirs her desire. It could indicate that this series of typical scenes took place at school, perhaps with a teacher as father surrogate. Yet they seem more like sewing work at home, and Anna's father is often referred to as a tailor. As the two worked together on sewing, he evidently leaned on her or let her lean on him in such a way that both their candles were lit and his goose, or tailor's iron, pressed on her atlas, a satiny fabric that sounds like *arse*. Of course, it may have been only a geography lesson in which he leaned on her atlas, but there seem to have been strong sexual overtones, as suggested by the "two ohs" (like mutual orgasm) or the possible reference to the reproductive organs as "sowing machine."

Officially, and perhaps consciously, for one or both participants, these scenes continued to be lessons or chores. One classic scene of this kind is in Nabokov's *Lolita* (60–63), where Humbert Humbert bounces Lolita on his lap before they become lovers, and she does not seem to be aware that he has an orgasm. The fact that ALP could not mention the erotic activity going on added to the pressure that the father figure exerted on her. At least she thought he was exerting such pressure, and the very undefined uncertainty of this sensation was exciting. In her letter, ALP recalls her early love for HCE as an archaic situation of uncertainty that she backed into when they were pals: "backed in paladays last, on the brinks of the wobblish" (*FW* 615.25–26). The image of a lost age framed unclearly, or in a wobbly

way, together with the Miltonic reference to a patriarchal Eden, suggests an infantile root.

A LOGIC OF POLARITY

If such scenes form ALP as a woman through subordination laced with
subornation, she reacts to her position on two levels: the level that is
contained by her role and the one that is not, or the ordinary and the
heroic. Lacan says in a discussion of tragedy that everyone includes
both: "In each of us the path of the hero is traced, and it is precisely as
an ordinary man that one follows it to the end" (*Ethics* 319). It may be
that in old age everyone approaches heroism and tragedy: Joyce indicates it in this chapter, citing the tendency of aging muscles to sag as a
prefiguration of death: "Heroes' Highway where our fleshers leave
their bonings" (*FW* 607.12–13).

I will look first at the level on which woman's position is compelling
to ALP, but the level on which she sees beyond this position will later
be emphasized as she moves outward to the limit of life. The two levels
coexist constantly in her discourse, which expresses both devotion and
irony. The two may be associated with the follower Doddpebble and
the creative Quickenough.

The level that is enclosed by woman's role follows the logic of polarity, which includes both submission to men and female aggression;
but female aggression may move beyond this logic. It is debatable
whether the level beyond active-passive polarity can be reached without passing through such polarity, both because rebellion requires aggressive reaction and because one can approach freedom from the
poles only through balancing them. Joyce portrays ALP so as to insist
that the logic of polarity is virtually inescapable, but he also sees that
her value, power, and beauty ultimately depend on her passing beyond this logic.

As a traditional woman, ALP is pitiful enough. She does not seem to
show resentment over the feelings imposed on her. Rather, she misses
the archaic form of the man who surreptitiously dallied with her: "Still
and all he was awful fond to me. Who'll search for *Find Me Colours*
now on the hillydroops of Vikloefells? . . . There'll be others but non so
for me" (*FW* 626.16–20). The phrase "fond to me" smooths over her
impression that the fondness was largely on her side. After switching
from the third person, which indicates the old form of her man, to the
second, which indicates the present form, ALP presents two vivid ver-

sions of the continuing pattern of the man pressing on her. The first is a peaceful vegetable love in which he is a tree, while the second is aggressively animalistic:

One time you'd stand fornenst me, fairly laughing, in your bark and tan billows of branches for to fan me coolly. And I'd lie as quiet as a moss. And one time you'd rush upon me, darkly roaring, like a great black shadow with a sheeny stare to perce me rawly. And I'd frozen up and pray for thawe. (*FW* 626.21–26)

The peaceful version seems to represent, or to evoke and make imaginable, the balance in which polarity is overcome. That an ancestral name for HCE, Finn MacCool, is involved in "fan me coolly" suggests that he expresses himself in the satisfaction he gets from making her happy. Undertones of the preposition "fornenst" may imply that they create each other. McHugh calls it a dialectal word for "over against," but I think there is also a play here on the German *vornehmen*, "take up," and possibly on a synthetic German word, *vornennen*, which (if it existed) would mean "name in advance or call forth." The last level would imply that HCE and ALP evoke each other. "Forenenst" was used in the letter to distinguish the peaceful HCE from the "thug" Sully, for HCE was seen as "gentle as a mushroom and a very affectable [which includes 'vegetable'] when he always sits forenenst us for his wet" (*FW* 618.26–27). This suggests that he always evokes her for his inebriation, his lubricity (or lubrication), and his wit (or intelligence).

The perfect mutual passivity described in these passages has long been a feminine ideal of love. It is referred to as "vegetable love" in Andrew Marvell's "To His Coy Mistress," but Marvell presents it as a woman's notion that the poem mainly opposes. His speaker maintains that since time presses, her coyness amounts to a "crime," and they should "at once" "tear" their "pleasures with rough strife." Simply in terms of enjoyment, the woman, who never speaks, may be right to feel that they would be better off taking their time. But her view is only "a side strain of a main drain of a manzinahurries" (*FW* 214.2–3), and the male view dominates.

Aristotle saw the vegetable aspect of the soul as lower than the animal, and the animal version of love that is contrasted to the vegetable in ALP's soliloquy takes the climactic position of emphasis because it is more decisive. What interests me about this brutal scene is ALP's reaction. The violent wound of his penetration ("perce me rawly") causes her to freeze before she can think, as implied by the sudden perfect tense: "I'd frozen up." "Pray for thawe" shows that having been rendered frigid by male brutality, the woman is then obliged to accept this brutality with reverence ("from the awe"); and to wish as devoutly as she can for a thaw that can come only from accepting humiliation and pain as exciting. Through such typical scenes, ALP recounts a training process by which the pattern imposed on her in childhood has been reiterated to make up some of her fondest memories. Joyce insists here on the common situation of women, who have been conditioned throughout history to find satisfaction on the verge of abuse.

To some extent ALP separates herself from this animal experience by describing it critically, but the inurement of womanhood is such that she remains attached to it on one level. Her tone here continues to be impressed by what she's been through, but notices its unfairness. Here we see her two levels: ordinary acceptance, which is caught up in the logic of polarity, and heroic irony, which seeks beyond it. Neither her susceptibility nor her disillusionment can win; in fact, each feeds and depends on the other. The rational way to handle such division is to have her ironic awareness control or ride her accepting side, and I will show signs of her adopting such an attitude at the end.

Similar divisions operate in all oppressed groups, who are obliged to get their satisfaction in ways defined as inferior. This is behind their mixture of laughter and tears, and Joyce brings this aspect in here through the analogy of the Irish as victims of colonialism. Just as ALP's personality has been defined by paternal intervention, so nationality is formed by foreign incursion. HCE is described here as "bark and tan," a reference to the dreaded British Black and Tan forces, and his aggressive connection with ALP is summed up as "The invision of Indelond" (FW 626.28). The inner vision of desire that occupies her is an invasion. And the Irish personality was formed by English invasions, which gave the Irish such fundamental components as their ordinary language and their rebelliousness. One of the early invading groups was the Vikings, and the pattern of dread they established is still being repeated on this page as "that wind as if out of norewhere!" (FW 626.4). The universality of such patterns is indicated by remembering that the English personality, often thought of as pure, was formed earlier by the invasions of such groups as the Angles and the Saxons, invasions that presumably contributed to the English drive toward conquest. In presenting the status of woman as colonized, Joyce implies that she should pass beyond that status, but he recognizes how difficult such a passage will be. For woman, as for Ireland, the declaration of freedom leaves mental bonds.

ALP became feminine and attractive by being made subject to male authority: "I was the pet of everyone then. A princeable girl" (*FW* 626.26–27). "Principal girl" is Dublin stage language for a "star," and ALP, who is proud of having been a pet, was "princeable" because she was capable of being princed. Moreover, she was conditioned to find attractive what was frightening: "And you were the pantymammy's Vulking Corsergoth. The invision of Indelond. And, by Thorror, you looked it! My lips went livid for from the joy of fear" (*FW* 626.28–29). The word "pantymammy's," based on pantomime, indicates that this vulgar, hulking, fucking Viking is just what the women want, and mothers train their sons to be served by women and treated as big shots; so the possessive may mean he's her product. We can see ALP's irony here, but also her emotion. Her shift from "for" to "from" shows her inveterate desire to look good by falsifying her native feelings, for it jumps from Irish dialect to proper English. Her "joy of fear" expresses the inseparability of desire from anxiety, and this is another childhood pattern that remains: "Like almost now" (*FW* 626.29–30). Yet the precise articulation of "almost" suggests that she may be putting this desire behind her as she claims herself by telling her story.

The force of ALP's disillusionment and rejection is shown by a late line: "All me life I have been lived among them but now they are becoming lothed to me" (*FW* 627.16). Here she realizes that she did not lead her own life: it was lived for her by others who partook of the system that made her a woman. The parallel between the passives "lived" and "lothed" indicates the inevitability with which she must come to loathe those who participate in the system that denies the activity of her life.

ANNACLITIC POWER

HCE's phallic authority was supposed to give ALP a center of meaning and causality that would articulate her feelings—"How you said how you'd give me the keys of me heart"—but now she finds that he was finally not able to: "Only, no, now it's me who's got to give" (*FW* 626.30–31, 32). One of the most disturbing things about him is his lack of real authority. He cannot originate feelings because of the static nature of the masculine function, so she realizes that emotionally he is her projection—which is one implication of her words "O mine!" (*FW* 626.32). But she cannot face the thought of his emptiness, so she is haunted by her responsibility for his activity: "But you're changing, acoolsha, you're changing from me, I can feel. Or is it me is? I'm getting mixed" (*FW* 626.35–36). As she begins to turn to salt water, she is losing her identity, and she can feel him losing his, turning to a fresh mate, as men often do. If she is fresh and he is salt, they are bound to have this effect on each other, which reduces differences that make them attract each other. She tends to blame something wrong with her for his straying. Yet she may also realize that she is finally outgrowing him.

In reaction to oppressive polarity, she is developing her aggressive side. Traditional psychoanalysis would see this as an internalization of a father figure, but what Joyce shows is more bisexual. When she says she thought HCE "great in all things," but he's only "a puny," she's comparing him to an old standard: "How small it's all!" (*FW* 627.23–24, 20). This standard does have a paternal aspect, and she blames HCE for being feminine when she complains of his "greedy gushes" and "lazy leaks" (*FW* 627.19–20). But she frees herself from the male standard by comparing him to feminine models. She turns back from his people to hers, women who were bold rather than petty. Her assertion of her independence leads to a lesbian vision of her dancing with a girlfriend of her youth who is described with a modifier usually applied to men: "How she was handsome, the wild Amazia, when she would seize to my other breast!" (*FW* 627.28–29).

I will return to this reunion and its feminine potential, but for now I want to focus on a problem involved in it. McHugh notes here that Amazons had one breast cauterized in order to shoot arrows better, and this emblematizes a dilemma: to assert the power of woman is to sacrifice a measure of womanhood because power is defined in phallic terms. Yet without advancing their power, women cannot claim or express their obliterated womanhood. They must set up a field of force to resist the domination of their minds by male images if they are to reach their own chapel of womanly feeling beyond active-passive polarity.

Joyce portrays ALP's self-assertion in her letter as an attack on man's feminine side, his rear end. She seems to get this idea from HCE and to direct it at Magrath, but the passage is unclear and may be directed at HCE. It begins as the letter starts to close: "Moral. Mrs Stores Humphreys: So you are expecting trouble, Pondups, from the domestic service questioned? Mr Stores Humphreys: Just as there is a good in even, Levia, my cheek is a compleet bleenk. Plumb" (*FW* 616.34–617.1). She asks if a servant or creditor, who could well be Magrath, will give trouble. He insists that his check is a blank, meaning that he cannot pay, he is plumb out of money. What follows is an extension of his statement that may be summed up in crude terms as "so fuck him":

"Meaning: one two four. Finckers. Up the hind hose of hizzars" (FW 617.2-3). "Finckers" are stinking fingers here, and "hind hose" is "rectal tube."[9]

Other readings, however, are possible: Rose and O'Hanlon (311) think that ALP asks HCE if the maid is pregnant by him, and he insists that he is innocent. His cheek is blank because he has nothing to blush about. In this case, it may be ALP who reacts in her letter to HCE's claim of innocence by wanting to goose him with a vengeance. Another reading is that when HCE says he never invaded the maid, ALP thinks he probably got the maid to invade him.

Whether or not ALP got this image from HCE, she certainly takes it over when she imagines her revenge on Magrath, who may stand for HCE's weak side. Her aggression symbolizes in gross terms the implicit power of her beauty to abase men, what Stephen calls "woman's invisible weapon" (U 9.461). The scene she conjures up is that of a mistress who brings in male brutes to beat her masochistic lover, as at the end of Sacher-Masoch's Venus in Furs. The brutes include not only cannonballs and Conan Doyle, both in McHugh, but Blazes Boylan and Conan (both the Irish hero and the pop barbarian). On a primary level they are canon boys, church officials who enforce the law:

Conan Boyles will pudge the daylives out through him, if they are correctly informed. Music, me ouldstrow, please! We'll have a brand rehearsal. Fing! One must simply laugh. Fing him aging! Good licks! Well, this ought to weke him to make up. (FW 617.14–18)

The brute expresses the woman's power, and in this passage she is symbolically putting fingers in Magrath (or HCE), showing that he is "weke" and "aging." He is so degenerate that he has to be goosed to get it up, and the reversal of "make him wake up" implies that she will weaken him to the point of using makeup.

ALP's phallic aggression, a sort of indirect female rape, leads to a "fooneral" for Magrath at which "Femelles will be preadaminant" (FW 617.20, 23). This is a return to a posited feminine level before Adam, or before the imposition of the patriarchal order. With the man gone, the women revert to the "languo of flows" (FW 621.22), the semiotic shift of jouissance that breaks down linguistic containment. The image of bursting out of language is prominent at the end when ALP reverts to her pre-male life of dancing among the seahags: "And the clash of our cries till we spring to be free. Auravoles, they says, never heed of your name!" (FW 627.31–33). In Latin the cries say, "You may fly [voles] the air [aura],"[10] so ALP is receiving here an inspiration much like Stephen's airborne feeling in chapter 4 of *Portrait*; and his cries, like hers, seek passage beyond existing forms. But like his, hers are subject to rational critique. The world before definition they aspire to can be found only retrospectively, with an aggressive motivation, in opposition to actuality: "But I'm loothing them that's here and all I lothe" (*FW* 627.33).

ALP's rebellion, insisting on independence, is a polarized reaction against entrapment and loss, against losing her countersign, HCE, and her own identity. On the last three pages she follows a shifting sequence as she leaves one signifier to project another. The independence asserted in the first phase of this shift generates senses of loneliness, vertigo, and separation as termination: "Loonely [loony] in me loneness. For all their faults. I am passing out. O bitter ending!" (*FW* 627.34–35). So the second phase of the shift projects a new illusion of authority, a new version of the Other based on the infantile image of the absent father. In Lacan's terms, when ALP feels the freedom to expand beyond form, her sense of justification involves an implicit assumption of paternal authority, without whose protection no concept of freedom could subsist or be intelligible.[11] The key feature of the Other is its radical unknowableness, here figured forth by the unmeasurable sea, which is called "infrahuman" in *Portrait* (*P* 148).

ALP is leaving what she knows to plunge into the unknown at the end when she goes back to her "cold mad feary father" (*FW* 628.2), the ocean. A line in one of Joyce's *Wake* notebooks equates this father with HCE's siglum: "old old old ⌐⌐" (*JJA* 36.117). Her ambivalence about the authority she projects is what sustains the two levels she has seen in HCE all along—the buried one and the strider. As Devlin points out (*Wandering* 177), she moves on the last page between a frightening Father Ocean in the third person and a figure she invokes for shelter in the second. Even the second person, however, is linked to the father in the line "Carry me along, taddy, like you done through the toy fair!" (*FW* 628.8–9). From a skeptical point of view, the protecting aspect of the man affords no escape from the overwhelming one, for they are both parts of the same structure. Now the one that had to be buried to maintain her autonomy is rising, and she seems to confuse the two men more than ever at the end. She goes back to "you," her cold father, till the size of "him," the ocean, makes her "saltsick" and she rushes into "your arms," which are "those therrble prongs!" (*FW* 628.1–5). The ambivalence of the passage is emphasized in a draft that reads, "makes me seesaw saltsick" (*JJA* 63.259). Her nausea at swallowing "seasilt" may suggest semen.

The need for authority is so unbearable that ALP struggles to withdraw to the gentle aspect of the male or into female companionship. But the assertion of freedom has to lead to a further level of authority, and the archaic aspect of the father returns: "Finn, again!" (*FW* 628.14). Even if ALP were to follow her little-developed lesbian impulses and mate with a woman, the issue of dominance would return, and with it the position of the father.[12] The strength ALP feels on her own is based on what she felt when she was carried by her father. And when she sees the giant god figure bearing down on her at the end, she dreads with longing that she will sink to worship.

ALP is drawn at the end from the actuality of her man to what he stands for, an archaic, multiple incomprehensibility—the Other that relates to him as any system of signs, with its ancient roots, does to the sign it defines. While she tries to leave love behind for self-assertion, she can only turn to a more extreme, abstract form of love, a love of the infinite. What she seeks in the union she dreads with the totality of the ocean of mind is not satisfaction, but being; and Lacan argues that the confirmation of being, which is impossible, is the ultimate goal of love (*Technique* 276).

In his notes to *Exiles*, Joyce says that love, as pursued by Richard, seeks "union in the region of the difficult, the void and the impossible" (*E* 114). Hugh Kenner (90–93) has shown an extensive, seven-point parallel between the endings of *Exiles* and the *Wake*, but he also says that the *Wake* is different: "The quality of Bertha's yearning is reproduced, but the soul is allowed finally to cast itself out on the ocean that gave it being."

As the last leaf of formulated language stops clothing ALP and becomes something she must hold (*FW* 628.6–7), she is stripped into complete exposure and the source of being is revealed as the giving of herself to impossibility. Because the self is formed by reflection, she can speak only by going through the circuit with the Other that indicates the goal of love. To escape from love is as impossible as to realize it fully. The tragic tone that dominates the soliloquy expresses this situation: ALP's voice speaks of going on though it moves toward its own negation, split between the ideal man and the threatening one. But this negation will lead to an enlargement in the next cycle as disintegration leads to a new language, a new reading as the last sentence becomes the first. The next reading may see Anna's situation as woman in more skeptical terms or more optimistic ones, but it will never fully escape the terror and pity that give her life and gender.

7

A Leap Past

ALP between Deaths

The patriarchal logic developed at the end of the previous chapter leaves ALP's hope of freedom doomed to remain unrealized in the intelligible world. But the *Wake* goes beyond this world, and the force of ALP's hope finally drives the book beyond doom toward progress. Joyce's major works end suspended between possibilities, and the grim picture I just sketched is far from covering the *Wake*'s final view of women, though it remains as part of that view.

The fulcrum for the forward movement of hope for ALP's womanhood is the recognition that once she sees through HCE and feels her feminine identity, this realization will not be wiped out by her dread of Father Ocean and his trident. Though she fears she will fall at the feet of the male spirit, she does not stop. On one level, as Ellmann notes, the "therrble prongs" into which she rushes are the North and South Walls of the Liffey, which form a bottleneck between the harbor and the Bay (*JJ* 712). But these she passes beyond.

It is true that they are followed by "Two more" (*FW* 628.5), but the prongs will not hold her because they cannot give her life. The clear reference to "tumor" indicates that they constitute the barrier of death. Joyce's mother died of cancer, and Nora was cured of it in 1929 (*JJ* 607). The series of imposing male images that flash before Anna on the last page as she leaves her accustomed role of woman behind are presented here as metastases when "Two more" is followed by "Onetwo moremens more." As mermen they are submerged in her mind, and as polygamous Mormons they are patriarchal. This barrage of visions of awesome men is a flak she must pass through, and the way she notices how

113

these men multiply implies that the swarm will not last. She is probably attempting to leave them behind with "Avelaval" (FW 628.6), which, as McHugh points out, includes the Latin *ave et vale*, "hail and farewell."

ALP deflects her mind from the threatening, pronged father to the gentler one who carried her at "Carry me along, taddy . . ." (FW 628.8). This may be seen as the pitiful delusion of a dying woman who sees father death coming for her; but it can also be read more positively as a sign that she is controlling her vision, that she can focus on the aspect of the father that is useful. She does not see him as a goal, but uses him to support her as she pursues her own womanly aim.

If men, as Winnicott argues, find the space to expand their imaginations in the field of the mother, women may find a similar creative abolition of distinctions sustained by the field of the father. In fact Kristeva, reversing Winnicott's genders, says that there has to be "a living and a loving father" in order for the child to create "a space of play" (cited in Grosz 159).

That the firmness of men is something women depend on to allow them to reverse and oscillate distinctions is suggested by a passage of ALP's memory from the first chapter, which follows the end. Here again sexuality figures forth the psychic interaction of genders and generations. The father as carrier taking young ALP to the fair shifts toward a lover so overwhelming her with his manual dexterity that she does not know up from down: "The lips would moisten once again. As when you drove with her to Findrinny Fair. What with reins here and ribbons there all your hands were employed so she never knew she was on land or at sea or swooped through the blue like Airwinger's bride" (FW 28.11–15).

On another level this passage says that men's hands control the machinery of power (reins) that provides women with protected space to let their feelings flow. This level may be called more primary and substantial than the incestuous sexual undertone of the passage, though such judgments are always questioned by the *Wake*. The meanings of these lines converge on the word *transport*, which means "to move, to enrapture, and to send to penal servitude," with the first meaning carrying the others.

This passage probably implies that if women held the reins, they might lose their ability to cultivate feminine sensitivity. On one hand, men may be seen as beasts of burden who allow women to be the main participants in the beautiful activities of life, yet on the other, the control that the man exerts keeps woman in an abysmal state of ignorance. The power of the father operates through support as well as abuse, and these two sides may be hard to distinguish. Insofar as ALP cannot separate the power of the father from the dream of the lover, she is trapped in the patriarchal myth of womanhood. Yet the first line quoted makes it clear that in middle age she is revivified by this memory. Of course, it is an idealized memory: the narrator says, "If you only were there to explain ..." (FW 28.10), even though HCE may very well be there.

Ellmann says, "The phrase, 'Carry me along, taddy, like you done through the toy fair,' was inspired by a memory of carrying his son George through a toy fair in Trieste to make up for not giving him a rocking horse" (712). I conjecture that Joyce carried Lucia similarly, for it is a common practice. A child may derive from such experiences a recurring sense of uplift, of having power and seeing far; and we should not disclaim such benefits because they may be accompanied by complications.

There are many stories of women being seized and flown through the air by lovers, from Leda and the swan to Lois Lane and Superman. The code behind such tales is seriously unfair in that it allows man to think of flying independently like Daedalus, while woman has to be taken up. But Joyce modifies this code radically. As I have noted, the voices of women preside over transcendence at the ends of all of Joyce's novels. In Portrait, Stephen has to make contact with the "womb" of his imagination, his feminine "chamber" (P 188), before he can take off: "See Capels and then fly" (FW 448.9). In the Wake, the ultimate source of flight is maternal.

A manuscript version of the ending includes lines later omitted that suggest that HCE keeps carrying ALP after the line about "taddy." The 1938 typescript, before corrections, reads, "I'm taller now. For all you're heavy. And there. As then. Bussofthee [,] mememormee! Lps. Take. The keys to. Given!" (JJA 63.262). It is not certain that HCE is carrying her in the first two sentences, for these were omitted at the same stage at which "Carry me along, taddy ..." was added. ALP may be returning to the image of them both walking. But I think that the connection involved in "I'm taller now. For all you're heavy" implies that she is a bigger burden now than she was as a child. The grotesque image of the old man carrying the grown woman, a possible reference to King Lear, shows a pitiful fixation, but her size makes her more dominant.

Her dependence on his susceptibility to carry her forward is parallel to the fact that Joyce's need for a superb or proud woman who would reject him is at the basis of his vision of woman's independence, her unfolding of her own mind. Oppressed groups have to use the weaknesses of their masters to gain strength, and Joyce becomes stronger as a creator by giving his creations more strength to defy him.

The last punctuated words of the Wake are "The keys to. Given!" They refer to Arrah-na-Pogue, which Glasheen (15) translates as "Nora of the Kiss," a play by Dion Boucicault in which the heroine has freed

her lover from prison by passing a message through a kiss. As the *Wake*
ends, Anna has delivered the letter that expresses her love for HCE,
but the last line also refers to a line two pages earlier: "How you said
how you'd give me the keys of me heart" (FW 626.30–31). At the end,
ironically, he may have given her the keys to her heart by disillusioning
her so that she is ready to set out alone on the last stage of her journey.

Putting "taddy" into service beneath her, ALP generally sees herself
on land in the last nine lines, carrying on the quest that I see as finally
aimed at the lost chapel of her womanly being: "There's where. First.
We pass through grass behush the bush to. Whish! A gull. Gulls. Far
calls. Coming, far!" (FW 628.12–13). Here the sound of the wings of the
gulls, "Whish," corresponds to wish fulfillment because this and other
bird sounds that echo through the soliloquy are parts of the song of
dawn. This sound emerges from a landscape that seems to be filled
with soft sounds: "pass . . . grass . . . behush . . . bush." And "Whish"
appears as the object of the quest by following "to." The noises of the
gulls signal that something is "coming," though it is "far." And this
power in the sky that the gulls announce is not a father but a mother.

In a notebook for the *Wake* Joyce wrote this version of part of the
ending:

> And it's old
> and old it's
> weary I go
> back to you,
> my cold father,
>   mother
> and old it's sad
> and old it's sad
> & weary mother
> I go back to you,
> my cold father
> my cold mad
> father, my cold
> mad bleary
> father, yet the sight
> of him makes me
> saltsick and I
> rush into your
> arms. (*JJA* 40.261)

The last dozen lines of this can be read as turning from father to mother
with the following sense: Mother I go back to you—my cold father

makes me sick and I rush into your arms. But this reading is strained and probably only a secondary suggestion. What is clearer is that Joyce originally intended ALP to rush into a sea that combined both parents, and perhaps the reason he removed the references to mother is that he decided to make her a separate goal.

When ALP was a child she was carried by a mountain, and now she will be carried by the sea; but this is not her goal or where she wants to stay. The terms of the last pages make it clear that ALP is bound to pass beyond the ocean she enters with such anxiety. Even the version of the father with "whitespread wings" on the last page will not hold her. He comes from "Arkangels" because as an angel he represents the Christian structure of heaven; but there is an alternative, maternal structure that is bound to replace this paternal one in ALP's mind. She will reach the body of the creative mother, though she can do so only by disintegrating. This mother is the sky goddess Nut. Before I show how ALP's flight up to Nut, the final stage of her journey, is portrayed in the *Wake*, I will prepare for it by explaining through Lacan's theory of tragedy the moral basis of ALP's final situation.

ALP BETWEEN TWO DEATHS

Through her division and her disillusionment, ALP ultimately assumes a tragic position between two deaths. Lacan distinguishes physical death from a second death that involves leaving the Symbolic order of language behind, and says that the tragic figure is between the two. His main example is Antigone, but he argues that for all of Sophocles' extant protagonists, with the possible exception of Oedipus, "the race is run" (*Ethics* 272). They are already in the zone between life and death because they have made their fatal choices by the time their plays begin. But it is this very doom which makes it possible for them to affirm their values. So we see them suffer their ends, and it is perceptive of Joyce to refer to Sophocles as "Suffoclose!" (*FW* 47.19)

Antigone, one of the most famous heroines to have a name starting with "An," places herself outside life by rejecting male authority (Creon) and the possibility of having a husband in order to be loyal to her own family doom. ALP finally rejects HCE as false, petty, and loathsome, so she turns back to her own people, who are women. This vision builds on the difference between fatherland, the place the husband's people come from (such as Joyce's Dublin), and motherland, which the wife's people are from (such as Nora's Galway). Moreover, as Chodorow (76–77) argues, the strongest emotional ties of women are often with women, whereas their relations with men are more tentative because men are apt to be limited in their responses to women's need for love.

ALP looks back on life in her youth dancing among "bold and bad" women (FW 627.25) whom she associates with a powerful sense of liberation: "Ho hang! Hang ho! And the clash of our cries till we spring to be free" (FW 627.31–32). Her life with women, which was drenched with erotic feelings, remains her strongest version of herself. Something approaching lesbian experience probably made women attractive to Joyce. Nora dressed as a boy in her teens (Maddox 18–19), and Molly enjoyed sleeping with Hester Stanhope, though they did not have sex: "she had her arms round me" (U 18.641–42). Molly also remembers that Bloom was jealous of her friend Floey Dillon because Molly spent so much time with her (U 18.184–85), and her friend Josie Breen used to embrace Molly when Bloom was there "meaning him of course" (U 18.203). These experiences, and Molly's closeness to Milly, enrich her vitality. In Joyce's case the appeal of women with a homoerotic component overlaps with an attraction to dominant women, but it may be that men generally, in their relations with women, derive satisfaction from the emotionality that women develop with other women.

ALP associates lesbianism with the idea of equality in love, and dreams of reconstituting her relationship with HCE on this basis. When she envisions their outing as an equalized dutch treat on a Dublin United Tramways Company tram to Howth, the sentence starts with a reference to lesbianism: "Les go dutc to Danegreven, nos?" (FW 622.20–21). Yet the Sapphic ideal is flawed by the return of the father: lesbians seeking escape from masculine aggression may find themselves haunted by butch-fem roles. But the idea of equality is worth striving for no matter how unattainable it may seem—and the vision of tragedy is not impaired by the impossibility involved in it. Consider the cases of Antigone and Lear, who is another example Lacan uses. It is easy to argue that both are foolish or pathological, but this does not stop them from expressing ideas of freedom and justice that stand for the hope of the future. Tragedy tends to argue that the truth has to appear impossible and insane in a world ruled by evil. The transcendent dimension of tragedy is marked by a quality that concentrates its greatest intensity in this genre of loss and suffering: beauty.

Beauty gives a woman aggressive or transgressive power as it goes beyond words to stop being involved in the Symbolic system or subject to the law. This is why Lacan says that beauty is the limit of the second death (*Ethics* 260). Antigone is located here in what Lacan calls the "unbearable splendour" of "this terrible, self-willed victim" (*Ethics* 247). As physical beauty exceeds language, spiritual beauty exceeds logic. This is where Anna is located as she turns against the ordinary world, and turns away from land to the companionship of waters. Irigaray (106–18) develops the opposition between solid masculine logic and fluid feminine thinking.

It is possible, though not clear, that the *Wake* refers to the heroine of Kate Chopin's feminist novel *The Awakening* (1899), Edna Pontellier, who rejects the men in her life and their treatment of her as property by swimming naked into the Gulf of Mexico. *The Awakening* stirred controversy and censorship at the turn of the century, so Joyce, who reviewed an American novel in 1903 (*CW* 117–18), might have heard of it; and he would have liked its sensuous prose and its thematic affinities with Flaubert and Ibsen. The third chapter of the *Wake* refers to ALP's death (and HCE's) as "Edned" (*FW* 54.5). Even if Joyce did not know of Chopin, the parallels between the *Wake* and the *Awakening* (both of which present versions of Ophelia) are significant. Chopin's novel ends with fragmentary impressions, including memories of her childhood and her father, streaming through Edna's mind as she enters the sea.

Water wears land away, and Joyce was partial to the tradition that beauty is stronger than power. This is implied in the Quinet passage that recurs in the *Wake* about flowers outlasting empires. In the "Ithaca" episode of *Ulysses*, Bloom thinks about the power of the moon: "her potency over . . . waters: her power to enamour, to mortify, to invest with beauty, to render insane . . ." (*U* 17.1163–65). Yeats's 1929 translation of a passage "From the 'Antigone'" emphasizes that her beauty and the beauty of her sacrifice, which demolish Creon and his son, have the force to overcome the whole male power structure:

> Overcome—O bitter sweetness,
> Inhabitant of the soft cheek of a girl—
> The rich man and his affairs,
>
> . . .
>
> Overcome Gods upon Parnassus;
>
> Overcome the Empyrean; hurl
> Heaven and Earth out of their places,
>
> . . .
>
> By that great glory driven wild.

Pray I will and sing I must,
And yet I weep—Oedipus' child
Descends into the loveless dust.
(276)[1]

With all her power, this beauty is doomed because her father is subject to the Oedipus complex. As David Bloom remarked, the main reason Antigone is outside the Symbolic order from the start is that as a
child of incest, she cannot fill a place in society. But as I have shown,
ALP is also haunted by incestuous overtones, and Gilbert indicates
that in a sense virtually every daughter is a child of incest insofar as
her beauty subjects her to the paternal desire to possess.

Lacan situates beauty on a scale of movement toward "the central
field of desire" (*Ethics* 217). This is the field of the Other, toward which
we are always moving, and we objectify the Other as the Thing, the
maternal object of desire. On this scale, "if the good constitutes the first
stopping place, the beautiful forms the second and gets closer. It
stops us, but it also points in the direction of the field of destruction"
(*Ethics* 217). We can neither stop aiming at the maternal object nor
reach it, and the closest we can come to reaching it is death. I believe that the good is the locus of the first, physical death, as beauty is
that of the second, Symbolic one. Lacan says that the good has authority over all exchanges between men, all Symbolic life. But something
becomes beautiful at the point at which it stops being good, goes beyond its function—an idea parallel to Stephen's notion of stasis
(*P* 179–80). In Irigaray's (110–11) terms, the feminine mechanics of flu-
ids, which is the substance of life and beauty, is excluded by the solid
logic of men.

Slavoj Žižek, the leading commentator on Lacan's *Ethics*, speaks of
the tragic space between deaths:

This gap can be filled in various ways; it can contain either sublime beauty or
fearsome monsters: in Antigone's case, her symbolic death, her exclusion from
the symbolic community of the city, precedes her actual death and imbues her
character with sublime beauty, whereas the ghost of Hamlet's father represents
the opposite case—actual death unaccompanied by symbolic death, without a
settling of accounts—which is why he returns as a frightful apparition until his
debt has been repaid. (135)

To be alive but outside the Symbolic order is to be beautiful; to be
dead but inside this order is to be horrible. The distinction between
Antigone and Hamlet senior seems to correspond to the gender roles,

with women excluded by the Symbolic order and men contained by it
at the expense of their physical sensitivity. In *Ulysses*, Leopold Bloom
was parallel to Hamlet senior as "a ghost by absence" (*U* 9.174). HCE
is seen as physically dead yet symbolically present and capable of waking in the first and last chapters of the *Wake* and at many points between. In fact, it has been shown that the *Wake* was influenced by the
anthropologist Stefan Czarnowski's account of burial customs among
the ancient Irish, according to which a hero's body would lie in public
for several days while contests were held to determine his legacy
(O'Dwyer). During this time, he would be regarded as provisionally
dead, his soul not yet having left his body, a formulation that accords
with Žižek and Joyce.

Anna possesses sublime beauty because she passes to the limit of the
second death by rejecting the Symbolic order. Beauty touches the second death because it rejects us: we cannot possess it or turn it into a
signifier. It is unspeakable, and because it breaks down existing language, it is the principle of creativity. Lacan says that by sweeping
aside "the reproduction of forms" that opposes nature's "possibilities," beauty forces "nature to start again from zero" (*Ethics* 260). At
this point he refers to de Sade's idea of a creative principle of crime
that passes beyond the existing order "to liberate nature from its own
laws" through transgression.

Lacan's thinking may be said to anticipate here the theories of
Gilles Deleuze and Félix Guattari in *Anti-Oedipus*. They argue that
society is organized around reproducing established forms, but the
real basis of the unconscious is a formless flow. In anti-oedipal terms,
the flow that ALP embodies is not womanly, but the original infantile and prehistoric flow of production that is repressed by social
forms. They argue that this flow is always revolutionary because it
disrupts codes (173). If women have, as Deleuze and Guattari say,
an "affinity with the germinal influx" (165), it is not because it is inherent in them, but because patriarchal society has delegated sensual-
ity to them and put them outside rationality in the position of the
Other.

Lacan says that Antigone's position relates to a criminal good, and
in this regard she represents rebellion. But *Antigone* is a systematically
feminist play, perhaps more than *Lysistrata*, which reconciles the genders. In the first scene, Ismene tells Antigone that because she is a
woman, she should not be defiant (Sophocles 165). Creon, whom Antigone defies and defeats, has these patriarchal lines:

No woman rules me while I live. (181)

They must be women now,
No more free running. (183)

So I must guard the men who yield to order,
Not let myself be beaten by a woman.
Better, if it must happen, that a man
should overset me.
I won't be called weaker than womankind. (186)

It seems he's firmly on the woman's side. (189)

Your mind is poisoned. Weaker than a woman! (189)

you woman's slave. (190)

His rationalism is inseparable from his misogyny. Irigaray (167–68), as part of her argument that women must be silenced as women to maintain the logic of patriarchal civilization, says that Antigone must be condemned to death to preserve rational law. And so the play suggests a level on which every woman represents a criminal good.

In a blisteringly feminist play, *The Duchess of Malfi* (1613), by John Webster, the Duchess says as they are about to strangle her for following her desires, "I would fain put off my last woman's fault" (4.2.215). She means that everything she did to express her feeling as a woman was wrong, and she'll be glad in a few minutes to free herself from the crime of being a woman—and she then tells her stranglers to pull strongly. Not only is woman's desire a crime, but she has a criminal good in her body, the thing that makes her a woman, and the term *das Ding* has sexual overtones in French as *la chose*. So every woman has a component of Antigone within her, a desire to reject the law of the father, which is what makes her beautiful.

Lacan maintains that to reject the name of the father leads to disaster, most likely madness, and he argues that after she is entombed, Antigone goes berserk before hanging herself (*Ethics* 299). ALP sees herself as a frenzied maenad when she joins her women "for all our wild dances in all their wild din" (*FW* 627.26–27). Tragic madness is necessary because it is generative, and Lacan argues that Aristotle is wrong to speak of a tragic heroine like Antigone as making a mistake (*Ethics* 277). By passing beyond the limit of the Symbolic, ALP affirms a new possibility, and Joyce chooses to end on this focus not merely out of compassion, but to affirm the hope of human freedom that her independence, like Antigone's, represents.

Žižek says that the place between two deaths is the site of *das Ding*, which he defines in terms which accord with Irigaray's view of women as what has to be denied in order to make the Symbolic order and history possible:

the real-traumatic kernel in the midst of the symbolic order. This place is opened by symbolization/historicization: the process of historicization implies an empty place, a non-historical kernel around which the symbolic network is articulated. (135)

Every historical system requires a center which is not subject to history. This is what Jameson, who agrees, refers to as the "absent cause" (82). HCE claims to embody this center, but his attempts to do so always collapse farcically. It is ALP whose unceasing movement comes closest to reaching the kernel of the Real, and as a woman passing beyond logical polarities, she may be said to reach it. She is the author of the letter that is the *Wake*, and her last sentence is its first sentence because by passing through negation she generates the progress of the work.

I have argued that by seeing ALP's final feelings, the reader is prepared to see the book in a new way. I do not deny that her love for HCE is important and that she remains attached to him on one level. One purpose of getting to know herself is to return to him in a more equal way. But the part of her that rejects him and continues her quest "a lone" as well as "a loved" on the last line is crucial to the forward thrust of the book and has been active all through the text.

In fact, because the *Wake*, as Joyce wrote Weaver in November of 1926, "ends in the middle of a sentence and begins in the middle of the same sentence" (*SL* 314), the beginning of the book springs from its ending. Therefore between ALP's final "the" and the "riverrun" that follows it to commence the *Wake*, she takes over the book's voice as a continuation of hers. She becomes again what she always has been as the author of the letter, the narrator of the whole thing, which simultaneously becomes on one of its main levels *Femagains Wake*. She maintains the lead she had gained at the end as the book opens with the river leading us to the castle.

ALP's takeover of the narration is an enactment of her reaching her goal and liberating herself and the reader. It also means that she is destined to keep going around with all the male conflicts in the *Wake*, but she will see "Sir Tristram, violer d'amores" waging his "penisolate war" (FW 3.4–6) from a woman's point of view. The feminine view (like those of other colonized subjects) is always present in the *Wake*, as it is in the ridiculousness of these lines; and if history follows the repeating design of the work, this view will probably be increasingly prevalent. I hope I am bringing my reader to a point from which (s)he can start reading all of the *Wake* with a useful perspective.

Through the progress of the work the feminine increasingly surrounds the masculine, encouraging laughter at male aggression and certainty. This redresses the imbalance between genders, allowing their relations to be reconstituted. Such reconstitution is a positive process in marriage conceived of as a rhythm of separation and reunion. Another enactment of ALP's goal is her unstoppable advance toward the maternal body of the Thing, and now that I have developed some of the moral and creative implications of her quest, I will show how she is bound to achieve her goal.

THE SKY MOTHER

From the start of her soliloquy, ALP is moving toward her lost chapel, the song of birds in the forest, the awakening of in-fancy: "The woods are fond always. As were we their babes in. And robins in crews so. It is for me goolden wending" (FW 619.23–24). The choirs of robins in the foolish ("fond") woods suggest through *Robinson Crusoe* the idea of a new, undiscovered world.

In fact, within the cluster of the song of dawn, robins form a motif of their own connected to the song "When the Red Red Robin Comes Bob Bob Bobbing Along," which was an enormous hit when Harry Woods wrote it in 1926. Many of the ideas of the song of dawn appear in "When the Red," which asserts, "There'll be no more sobbing when he comes throbbing his old, sweet song," and calls on humanity to "wake up" and "cheer up."[2] The *bob*, which means both a jerky movement and the refrain of a song, is a model for the movement of history in the *Wake*, and I have observed it in both ALP and HCE. In her case, Biddy's bead "went bobbing" (FW 214.1), while he appeared as a message in a bottle "With a bob, bob, bottledby" (FW 624.2), which was originally "bob bob bottledy bob" (*JJA* 63.211). (See also FW 480.30–32.) The birdbrained nature of this song has to keep it parodic on one level, and serves to remind us that images of hope in the *Wake* are always partly satires on that human tendency.

Another song about the arrival of a figure from the natural world who shakes things up is "The Wild Man of Borneo," which Gifford and Seidman describe formally as "a progressive street rhyme: 'The wild man of Borneo has just come to town. / The wife of the wild man of Borneo has just come to town' and so on through potentially endless improvisations" (403). The last line of the published version, which Ulrich Schneider sent me, is "The wind that blew through the whiskers on the flea in the hair on the tail of the dog of the daughter of the wife of the Wild Man from Borneo has just come to town" (see Bauerle 95).

Here, in a racist parody of society news, the Third World confronts Western civilization, and the multiplying of details suggests that the arrival of the Wild Man is momentous. Edward W. Said says that the appearance of the Semitic Bloom at the center of *Ulysses* "testifies to a new presence within Europe. . . . now instead of being *out there*, they are *here* . . ." (188).

One passage that takes the rhythm of "The Wild Man" is "*the abnihilisation of the etym*" (FW 353.22), the climactic nuclear fission of the Tavern chapter: "*the grisning of the grosning of the grinder of the grunder of the first lord of Hurtreford expolodotonates through Parsuralia*" (FW 353.22–24). This suggests that the appearance of the Wild Man is a sort of "Second Coming," a cataclysmic upheaval for the West, and I will show how this disruptive song is linked to some of the sea imagery that appears at the end.

To return to the robins, they sing for a wedding that is a walking. McHugh points out that "me goolden wending" refers to a line spoken by Stephen's mother's ghost when she appears in a torn bridal veil in "Circe": "I was once the beautiful May Goulding" (U 15.4173–74). Like Antigone, Anna is headed for a wedding in which her name will be her maiden name, her own name. She still calls on HCE, but the beauty of her last appeals has to do with the increasingly obvious fact that he will not reply. The chapel she approaches is her own body, as represented by her mother's.

The identification of the mother's body with the song of dawn is indicated in a version of this pattern by Cixous that appears in passages cited by Moi (114, 118). It is unlikely (though not impossible) that this personal vision of Cixous's was influenced by Joyce, so Cixous shows how the whole complex can appear in a woman. She says that for the preoedipal baby, the mother's voice is "a song before the Law" (114). That is, before the male categories of Symbolic language were imposed on it, the child would have to hear the mother's voice as music. Cixous identifies this song with milk and with the presence of the mother's body. The images of birds and dawn also become attached to it. Cixous says that "the Mother's Voice" returns to her continually, and that sometimes it seems to come from above when she wakes: "To be lifted up one morning, snatched off the ground, swung in the air. . . . To find in myself the possibility of the unexpected. To fall asleep as a mouse and wake up as an eagle! What delight! What terror. And I had nothing to do with it. I couldn't help it" (118). Here the feeling of entering the sky is that of being within the mother.

The idea of a daughter's being permanently inside her mother's sex organ is manifested when ALP refers to Issy as "swimming in my hindmoist" (FW 627.3). She says that since HCE has turned his desire toward his daughter, he can have her: "Be happy, dear ones! May I be wrong!" (FW 627.6). The last line indicates that she expects the impertinent Issy to make him miserable, so the following one suggests that ALP did the same. Perhaps her allegiance to her mother gave her a basis for seeing the limitations of men: "For she'll be sweet for you as I was sweet when I came down out of me mother. My great blue bedroom, the air so quiet, scarce a cloud. In peace and silence. I could have stayed up there for always only. It's something fails us. First we feel. Then we fall" (FW 627.7–11). "Me mother" uses Irish dialect to identify the two women with each other, and this sky womb is obviously where ALP was happiest (or thinks she was), and certainly where she is bound. Her uneasy situation with HCE seems to her temporary, but she could have stayed forever in the space of the mother, a strong expression of fondness.

This mother on high is the Egyptian sky goddess Nut (with the vowel sound of bush), whose separation from the embrace of her husband Seb (or Geb), the earth, produced the world (Budge cii). Therefore she is the original source of the Nile, one of the recurring goals of the Wake. It is notable that her creativity involved separating from her man. She was separate from earth during the day, but descended to him at night, creating darkness, and she swallowed the sun every night and gave birth to it in the morning (Ions 49). She also gave birth to Osiris, who is linked to HCE, and to Isis and many others. Her sky womb was thought to be the place people went to after death (Bishop 106); and she was depicted, naked and voluptuous, with arms outstretched, inside the lids of sarcophagi (Fig. 3), presumably so the dead could ascend into her. I do not know if Nut can be related to some ancient matriarchy, such as feminists find among the Sumerians (see Scott, James Joyce 95), but she does play a more active and imposing role than any female in the Judeo-Christian tradition.

Egyptian mythology is prevalent in the Wake, perhaps because Joyce felt that it was so remote that it was in little danger of being believed,

Figure 3. The sky goddess Nut on the underside of the lid of the sarcophagus of Princess Ankhnes-neferibre, Thebes, c. 525 B.C. Photo courtesy of the British Museum.

127

but surely because he recognized its importance as a primary source. If Antigone and Nut seem unrelated, it should be observed (though Joyce probably didn't know it) that the Oedipus myth, like the Judeo-Christian one, may well have been based on Egyptian sources.[3]

ALP describes the letter she has gathered, which stands among other things for all of literature, as "scrips of nutsnolleges I pecked up me meself" (*FW* 623.32–33). Here her knowledge of Nut is knowledge of herself. In fact, "up me" suggests that she found this knowledge in her vagina, and this turns out to be one location of Nut, whom Joyce sees as immanent as well as transcendent. Perhaps this is why certain crucial passages about Nut are buried in the heart of the *Wake.* "Nuttings on her wilelife!" (*FW* 113.3), a variant of "not on your life," is used to describe the hen finding the letter, and Bernard Benstock observes that this refers to Nut "who lays the Cosmic Egg" (144). This is a way of indicating that the perceived world comes from inside woman's body. The passage about "nutsnolleges" directly precedes ALP's formation of HCE out of language as the "hardest crux ever" (*FW* 623.33–34), so it is on the basis of her knowledge of her mother that she forms him. In the Lesson chapter (II.2), the main lesson Shem (Dolph) tries to teach Shaun (Kev) is that the place we all come from is "the whome of your eternal geomater" (*FW* 296–97), an embarrassing truth that Kev rejects violently.

The sky is associated in the *Wake* with feminine attraction, and with Issy, who is sometimes a cloud (*FW* 157.8–23). Perhaps Issy is linked to Nut because childhood leads back to mother, but the first description of Issy in the book describes Nut, whose body was decorated with stars: "(O my shining stars and body!) how hath fanespanned most high heaven the skysign of soft advertisement! But was iz? Iseut?" (*FW* 4.12–14).

The song of the naughtingels (nutangels?) associates Nut with the music of women as birds in the sky: "May song it flourish (in the underwood), in chorush, long may it flourish (in the Nut, in the Nutsky) till thorush! Secret Hookup" (*FW* 360.14–16). "Under-wood" is a title Ben Jonson gave to a group of his musical lyrics, and suggests that the feminine song of the nightingales is an undercurrent related to their interior "secret hookup."[4] McHugh connects this passage to the inscription on the tomb of Pepi II, which says that his name should flourish as long as that of Nut. The passage also plays on the return of Horus, and on Sekhet hetep, the Egyptian Elysian Fields. The affirmation of Nut's position replaces man's abstract kingdom in the sky with woman's sensual singtime, which, unlike the former, is temporary.

The Greek name that Plutarch gave to Nut, Rhea (Budge xlix), may also be referred to in the *Wake*. A matchmaker praises ALP to the Norwegian captain who seeks her hand (a version of HCE) by saying that there was "never a Hyderow Jenny the like of her lightness at look and you leap, rheadoromanscing long" (*FW* 327.10–11). While this praises her sexual abilities, saying that she can start quickly and make it last a long time, it also refers to the fact that hydrogen is the lightest element, and this fact seems to be connected in Joyce's mind to the way water rises when it evaporates.

I have said that Issy embodies ALP's hope, and Issy gives a complex description of the ascension to Nut in the Games chapter on the page before her militant declaration of the right of women to pleasure, which I cited in my Introduction. Issy is telling Shaun how attractive she is here by praising her mirror girl Maggy:

my wholesole assumption, she's nowt mewithout as weam twin herewithin, that I love like myselfish, like smithereens robinsongs, like juneses nutslost, like the blue of the sky if I swoop for to spy's between my whiteyoumightcal- limbs. (*FW* 238.27–30)

Elaborate connections are mapped out here. Issy's contact with herself through another woman is equated with the Assumption, in which the Virgin Mary flew up to heaven. Issy loves herself as she loves the song of the robin, which is linked to disintegration by "smithereens." Moreover, the disintegrating robinsong is tied to the ascension to the lost Nut sky, the ascent of the spirit to the mother. And the blue of the sky is equated with what Issy has between her legs. As what you might call limbs, these legs are sensational, but they are shrouded in uncertainty as whatdoyoucallems. Irigaray says to women, "The sky isn't up there: it's between us" (213).

The whole complex of the song of dawn, then, is contained within women, and all of this is compared to "juneses nutslost," a lost youth (*la jeunesse*) in the realm of Nut, the lost infantile communion with the mother, a fusion in which she was not separate, "nowt mewithout." McHugh, however, points out that *nutzlos* is German for "useless," and this indicates that the visionary world of fulfillment in woman is rendered nugatory—or nuts—by male logic, just as Issy's attractions are here being paraded before the vulgar Shaun. It seems that only after a lifetime of experience with gender oppression will Issy as ALP be ready to pass beyond this commerce into a reclaiming of the chapel within her.

Logically enough, ALP sees herself as reaching the body of the mother by dancing with women. As Henke (203) indicates, the women she sees herself dancing with near the end are waters. Rivers have often been seen as women throughout history, and Amazia and Niluna are the Amazon and the Nile, whom she will mix with in the ocean. Irigaray (111) finds an indication of women's mentality in the fact that they can mix to almost complete fusion. We can now see more implications in the last dance ALP envisions: "How she was handsome, the wild Amazia, when she would seize to my other breast!" (*FW* 627.28–29). Skeat says that *handsome* originally meant "dexterous," or good with one's hands. A woman may know how to handle a full breast well because she has them, though we shouldn't forget HCE's paps. The "other breast" Amazia handles amazingly well is an imaginary one, the breast of the body ALP might have had if she were free to consort with women.

The lack of such close communion was a major problem with HCE. One of the passages that indicates why she is fed up with him is "Yed he never knew we seen us before. Night after night" (*FW* 626.20). He had no sense of her awareness of herself, her continuous self-intimacy. Irigaray (151) says that because woman must reflect man, she cannot be allowed by the male economy to reflect herself. Unlike Bloom with Molly, HCE was unable to put himself into ALP's mind, and perhaps he seemed never even to remember that they had met previously.

Now she has left him behind on the surface of the sea, though what he represents cannot be left completely. The movement of the waves of the sea was associated earlier with the song of dawn in a Tavern passage celebrating marriage. Here the rhythm of "The Wild Man of Borneo" suggests that the freeplay of water is a liberating force associated with the other world and with the subversive power of laughter: "Though Toot's pardoosled sauve l'humour! For the joy of the dew on the flower of the fleets on the fields of the foam of the waves of the seas of the wild main from Borneholm has jest come to crown" (*FW* 331.32–36). McHugh points out that the first sentence is based on "Tout est perdu fors l'honneur." If all is lost but humor, the crowning of the wild man as mock king overturns established values; and the gorgeous anna-pests unfold the rich expanse of the female element of life that covers most of the globe with its endlessly shifting delight. In an early treatment of the *Wake*'s rhythm, William Troy (304) concluded that the book's "predominant foot" was the anapest, which he linked to Anna.

The lines that express the exultation of the maenads take on new meaning as a seascape of waves: "For 'tis they are the stormies. Ho hang! Hang ho! And the clash of our cries till we spring to be free. Auravoles, they says, never heed of your name!" (FW 627.30–33). For the Egyptians, storms occurred when Nut came close to the earth. so "stormies" would be her agents, or parts of her. "They says" indicates that they fuse. "Ho hang!" captures the movement of the waves as they hang suspended, and their rhythm is in "And the clash of our cries till we spring to be free." The accented last word of each of the anapests— *clash, cries, spring,* and *free*—has a spraying sound and a meaning that expresses the uncontrollable movement of water. The waves clashing together send up spray, and the spray, by disintegrating, visualizes and promotes evaporation. The word "till" shows Anna's awareness that her sojourn in the ocean will last only till she springs into the air to rejoin Nut. And "auravoles," which is what the wild waves are saying, means "you may fly the air."

This passage has grown as it has been reexamined, as *Wake* passages tend to do. One of my main points is that a continuing dimension of such growth is a strong understanding of the personal needs of women; and I believe that there are many more feminist insights (as well as insights in other areas) to be found in the *Wake*.

ALP's final union is not with her father, but with her mother. The ultimate aim of her desire combines the freedom of the female body with the loss of symbolic identity and the flight toward the mother. This leap is tragic, but it is supported by the circular dream structure of the *Wake* so as to indicate that on one level it is simply waking up, which is dying to the identity that one dreamed of and its network of imaginary social connections. In this sense ALP is only being herself as she leaps into the sky to overturn the phallocentric cosmography, and being herself is all the more real for being so strange and unlikely.

8

Conclusion

Annual Increments

At the ends of the first and last parts of the *Wake*, feminine voices that had been devoted to patriarchy grow disillusioned: they perceive that the father never returns or wakes up because the phallic position ultimately cannot be filled. These flowing female voices finally swell to mock and drown out masculine discourse, yet the longing for the male position never disappears. The feminine stream at the end is not capable of being a viable discourse without relating to masculine fixity because the semiotic needs the Symbolic. Nevertheless the feminine has to move beyond the masculine for progress or new ideas, and ALP's assumption of the narrative at the end carries us into the next revolution of the *Wake*.

Of course the place of feminism in the *Wake* depends on the values one brings to the book. Poststructuralist values, which emphasize the breakdown of authority, identity, and gender through the shifting of language, tend to put Anna and her daughter in a central position. For while all characters in the *Wake* tend to use language that shifts, the men try to hold fast, while the women enjoy the flow. The textual displacement of language opposes masculinity, but is at the heart of the feminine.

An indication of the position of feminism may be seen in the fact that Joyce puts ALP's awakening at the very end—or as something anticipated after the end. This may be explained through Mill's argument that freedom for women is the last form of freedom. In all other areas, the principle that might makes right is recognized as false; but in the dominance of men over women, oppression is concealed by the emotional connections involved (Mill 6–7, 16). Therefore Anna's waking is the ultimate one for humanity, and her replacement of patriarchy by matriarchy is a final level of enlightenment from this point of view—or the crucial step toward a final rapprochement of the genders.

I do not claim, however, that feminism is the ultimate or real meaning of the *Wake*. Views of the *Wake* set out in all directions, and phallocentric interpretations can be and have been written. But I have shown that radical feminism in the *Wake* forms an elaborate and carefully articulated system. This system is incisive in portraying the oppression of women and vigorous in affirming the hope of their liberation. And it represents a substantial component of Joyce's mind.

While Joyce's motives as a male feminist are questionable, this adds to the force of his vision of women, for it shows that even a man with mixed feelings can be angry at the treatment of women and inspired by their potential. Though the forces that blind the genders to each other can hardly be overestimated, we should support the most penetrating indications that men and women are capable of understanding each other. For me, the aim of education is to understand the opposite view; and this goal never stops being difficult, because when something is understood, a new opposition lies beyond it.

One reason men and women are capable of realizing each other's minds is that each contains both genders. Their male and female identities are drawn from the common interchange that I call the femasculine obsubject and that Joyce designates by the almost invisible term chapel. But the startling extent to which each gender includes the other should not make us forget the difficulty each has in recovering the other: the established gender codes involve so much suppression, repression, and distortion that it is almost impossible to recover the other gender we contain. Moreover, Irigaray (124–25) argues that womanhood is what is most suppressed, and makes up much of what psychoanalysis calls the unconscious. Joyce's struggles to recover the unconscious and the truth about the sexes have yielded a continuing source of revelation, and there is room to advance into his understanding of women. There is also plenty to be said about his misunderstanding of them, which I have only touched on.

I emphasize that Joyce's desire to conquer women, while it persists in many forms, may be no stronger than his desire to be rejected by them, to be shamed before them. While this latter desire served the development of his own subject through the projection of a sublime object, it also led him to see not only woman's suffering and exaltation, but her defiance of patriarchy and her glimmerings of a vision of her reality apart from men.

Nevertheless, while the tragic alienation of women speaks against the established order, there is a sentimentality in Joyce's focus on the terror and pity of Molly and Anna. A man can get deep satisfaction from pitying women, but this may not stop him from taking advantage of them. Joyce's view of women must be seen critically, but he himself practiced such criticism. His culpability as a subject in the patriarchal order is most sharply defined by Yared's suggestion that he sacrifices Anna to a project that finally cannot escape being male. As in the case of Antigone, however, her being sacrificed need not keep her from being a heroic expression of the side of women; and tragic women authors such as Emily Brontë and Woolf also sacrifice heroines.

If there are any number of viewpoints in the *Wake*, Joyce's belief in dialectics, based on Bruno, sees feminism as involved with its opposite. My last chapter delineated some of the *Wake*'s strongest feminist lines of development or thrust. But in my previous chapter, I presented Joyce's logical proof that women's dreams of liberation were based on delusion because the power of the father was inescapable. Thus the feminism I finally traced was already seen through an opposition that had established that it could not be held as a unified truth.

Because feminism, like any other theme, is so scattered in the *Wake*, strong linear thinking had to be used to recover it. By assuming provisional authority, I was able to show new, wide-ranging connections, to develop links between feminism and freedom. It may be better to make authority obvious than to pretend that one can do without it, and so end up claiming greater authority. But the feminism I posed against opposition has no chance of standing as the center of the work.

The possibility of liberation cannot be delineated without partaking of the logic of entrapment; but, on the other hand, logic cannot sustain itself without the motivation of freedom. While the feminine may have to return to the masculine, women will remain obliterated unless they strive for release. Their thrust for freedom grows stronger as it grows more tragic, as it grapples with its own impossibility.

The breaking free of the Symbolic system that takes place in virtually every line of the *Wake* is a movement toward feminine life that draws the text forward. This movement is bound to leave behind remains that are either dead stones or trees only partly alive. Those remains have their place in the framework needed to give the flux direction. But it is the movement that carries forward the hope of newness, the song of dawn.

The construction of gender is so deeply rooted in culture that it can be changed only by slow, incremental work in progress combining the flow toward freedom with the fixation of form. What is accomplished may be referred to as annual increments. The Latin *annus*, "year," refers to what goes around, as suggested by the English *annular*, "of a ring." Every time we go around with Anna by reading the *Wake*, she increases her power, as indicated by her taking charge of the narrative between the end and the beginning. For several decades now, the *Wake* has been read from increasingly feminine perspectives, a trend likely to continue. If this increase in woman's power in the *Wake* is in line with history, it fits Joyce's desire to be prophetic. He meant to present history as progress through literary work; and insofar as feminine values are linked to freedom through the disintegration of stable identity, it is histereve, with woman as its leader.

Notes
Works Cited
Index

Notes

Chapter 1. Introduction: Joyce toward Women

1. For a description of many of the Lacanian studies of Joyce, see my introduction to "Joyce between Genders." The first application of Irigaray to Joyce was Annette Levitt's; other critics who make use of Irigaray are McGee, whom I discuss below, and Leonard.

2. Sharp analyses of the feminist insight in *Dubliners* appear in Kershner and in Leonard, who makes brilliant use of Lacan's theories.

3. Cixous's dissertation led to her 760-page *Exile of James Joyce*, while Kristeva has often written about Joyce as exemplary. See Kristeva's *Desire in Language* (92) or her "Joyce the Gracehoper." It is relevant that the *Wake* was written in Paris.

4. Derrida speaks in "Two Words for Joyce" (148–50) of Joyce's strong influence on a series of his works. In "*Joyce le symptôme* I," in Jacques Aubert's collection *Joyce avec Lacan* (22), Lacan says that as a young man he met Joyce, and after that he often thought of his work. For discussion of Lacan's talks on Joyce, see the index of my *Veil of Signs*. Attridge (30 n. 9) notes the influence of Joyce on Lacan, Derrida, Cixous, and Kristeva.

5. Devlin, "Castration and its Discontents" and "Pretending in Penelope." Cheryl Herr was the first to emphasize Molly's role playing. Irigaray sees deliberate feminine mimicry as a useful step (76), but later has doubts about its ultimate value because it plays conventional roles (133).

6. Joyce's works also address other individuals, such as his brother Stanislaus, but I think that Mary Joyce was the main addressee; certainly she was on an emotional level.

7. The *Wake* has four Roman-numbered parts that begin on pages 1, 217, 401, and 591. It is customary to identify each chapter by Roman part number followed by the Arabic number of the chapter in that part.

8. The two best guides to the *Wake*, both by pairs of authors, present typical praise. Rose and O'Hanlon speak of "the most celebrated chapter in the *Wake*, 'Anna Livia' " (113), while Campbell and Robinson call Anna's final monologue "one of the great passages of all literature" (355).

9. Page and line numbers of McHugh's *Annotations* exactly correspond to those of the *Wake*. So this point is on 239.16 in McHugh, and there is usually no

need to give page numbers for McHugh. References to McHugh will be to this volume unless otherwise stated.

10. See my essay on this pattern, "The Disjunctive Structure of Joyce's *Portrait*," in *P* 251–67.

11. Future references to pages of this collection of pieces by Lacan and his *école* will be preceded by *FS*. This essay also appears in *Écrits* 281–91.

12. I am indebted to Scott's idea of "Myths of Female Origins."

13. There are several varieties of myrtle, and while some are too soft for flagellation, some are not. The *OED*, which mentions that the myrtle is sacred to Venus and an emblem of love, refers to myrtle trees, twigs, wands, and rods.

Chapter 2. Two Songs

1. Joyce uses the story of Gideon, from the sixth chapter of Judges, as a motif in II.3, the Tavern chapter. See the entry under Gideon in Glasheen's *Census*, which explains where and how different names are referred to in the *Wake*.

2. Derek Attridge (10–23) uses part of this passage to show the richness of possibility one encounters in reading the *Wake*. He says all readings can be valuable, but none can be definitive (23).

Chapter 3. The Voice of the River

1. McHugh notes that this refers to a famous quote from Henri IV, "Paris is worth a mass" (French *messe*). The great French king converted from Protestantism to Catholicism in 1593 to secure his position. Since he was assassinated in 1610, the question may be raised as to whether it was worth it.

2. Herbert S. Strean (124), an authority on sexuality, writes that in 1980 it was estimated that about 60 percent of married men had committed adultery, and about 35 percent of women. *Exiles, Ulysses,* and the *Wake* suggest that Joyce saw adultery as prevalent.

3. "Shis" and "hrim" appear on *U* 15.3103. In combination with the well-known *(s)he*, these pronouns should prove useful for describing figures whose genders are ambiguous or dual. To expand on what I have said here, we may say that shis gender is a dream of shis in the sense that what dreams or wakes our conscious minds probably has no gender, but it seems to resemble the feminine as what consciousness controls. The *Wake* builds heavily on the indistinguishability of sleeping and waking.

4. Rabaté, as part of his argument on the fundamental bisexuality of the *Wake*, speaks of HCE's nursing (180).

Chapter 4. Afric Anna: Joyce's Multiracial Heroine

1. Scott is struck by this line in a note in *James Joyce* (106), but does not connect it to other indications of ALP's negritude.

2. Lindsay refers to Mumbo Jumbo as a god of the Congo. Ishmael Reed, in

Mumbo Jumbo (7), cites a definition of the Mandingo original on which *mumbo jumbo* is supposedly based: a magician who vanquishes bad spirits. Reed's influential novel builds on the spiritual power this implies.

3. Campbell and Robinson (5n) argue that Spengler informs the historical structure of the *Wake*.

Chapter 5. Going to the Chapel

1. I have been influenced by Vicki Mahaffey's "'Minxing marrage and making loof': Anti-Oedipal Reading," which speaks of the celebratory and destructive aspects of marriage in the *Wake*. I agree with Mahaffey, but we focus on different details.

On another level, "Minxing marrage and making loof" refers to a pair of sins everyone commits, urinating and defecating. McHugh notes that *minxit* is Latin for "he urinated," while the second part connects "making" to both *loo* and *loaf*.

2. The standard derivation is in Skeat, but I got more data from Webster's *Third New International Dictionary*.

3. Van Mierlo found the notes Joyce took from Maitland in notebook VI.B.2, pp. 32–37. He is the one who added the "ies" to "bolsh" below.

4. Marina Warner, in a review of John Boswell's *Same-Sex Unions in Premodern Europe*, says that "homosexuality was proscribed with unprecedented virulence" (8) in 390, when Martin was seventy-four. Warner says that Boswell tries to prove that the Church originally gave its "blessing" to same-sex unions.

5. McHugh says that this refers to Psalm 68.18: "Thou hast led captivity captive"; but the verb form here, combined with references to Deborah elsewhere, shows that this passage refers to her "lead thy captivity captive" (Judges 5.12). David, who is credited with this psalm, took the line from Deborah, who came earlier.

6. Gottfried left his poem incomplete around 1210, a year in which there was a wave of violent reaction against heresy throughout central Europe relating to the Albigensian Crusades. See my "Instinct in Tristania."

7. Barbara Brivic points out that the chapel of eases is also a chapel of feces, and that this corresponds to creativity because finger painting with feces is a creative activity of infants.

Chapter 6. The Terror and Pity of Love: ALP's Soliloquy

1. From an unpublished translation by Kevin Z. Moore. The original is in Aubert 35.

2. A point made by Mort Levitt at our *Wake* reading group.

3. In *Ulysses* this line is rendered "wed her second, having killed her first" (*U* 9.679), and "weda seca whokilla farst" (*U* 15.3853).

4. Norris, in "The Last Chapter" (13–16), argues that by insisting that

Stephen Dedalus be a good boy, his mother threatens to extinguish his personality, and that this pattern is reflected at the end of the *Wake*.

5. The hero of Thomas Flanagan's splendid novel about the Revolution of 1798, *The Year of the French*, has seen many of his friends hung, and spends the entire novel trying to avoid this fate.

6. Compare *Portrait* 107: "The foul long letters he had written in the joy of guilty confession . . . only to throw them under cover of night among the grass in the corner of a field or beneath some hingeless door or in some niche in the hedges where a girl might come upon them as she walked by and read them secretly." It seems to me that such hidden confession always remained a component of Joyce's work.

7. *Brewer's Dictionary* (241) says that in nineteenth-century England the name Clark was associated with being dressy and affected, like a fancy clerk or "Nobby Clark."

8. Polhemus explains passages on Daddy Browning and Peaches (mainly *FW* 65.3–33), a prominent Wakean example of the relation of an old man to a young woman. Another perceptive treatment of the incest theme is Marilyn Brownstein's "The Preservation of Tenderness" (Friedman 225–56).

9. This passage was pointed out at our reading group by Dick Beckman, who is preparing a study of the important motif of fingers up in the *Wake*.

10. Martha Davis pointed out at a group reading that there seems to be a reference here to the story of Cephalus and Procris in book 7 of Ovid's *Metamorphoses*. Cephalus calls for a breeze while hunting, crying, *"Aura veni"* (breeze come). His wife Procris thinks he is calling to another woman, and this results in his accidentally killing Procris.

11. See my *Veil of Signs* 19–20, 71–72.

12. For Lacan, the position of father may be filled by a woman, but it cannot be escaped with impunity. Catherine Clément sums up Lacan's view in *The Lives and Legends* (170): "If the father, present or not, fails to occupy the symbolic position assigned to him by our culture, disaster ensues." The form this disaster is most likely to take is insanity.

Chapter 7. A Leap Past: ALP between Deaths

1. Yeats 276. This is the last poem of a series, "A Woman Young and Old," and is a free translation of lines spoken by the chorus, starting on line 880 of the *Antigone*.

2. The wide prevalence of this song as an image of hope is suggested by the existence of a complete Communist version, "When the Red Revolution Comes Bringing the Solution Along," which includes lines like "Rise up, you proletarians; stop acting like seminarians." Roz Melnicoff, who sang it for me, does not know how far back it goes.

3. In fact, both myths may have originated with the intellectual Pharaoh Akhnaton, who ruled around 1360 B.C. Freud argues in *Moses and Monotheism*

(1939) that Moses was an Egyptian priest who used the Hebrews to carry on Akhnaton's suppressed idea of monotheism. Immanuel Velikovsky claims in *Oedipus and Akhnaton* (1960) that the Pharaoh himself was the original model for Oedipus. Both books are highly controversial, but probably are correct in indicating some measure of Egyptian influence.

4. Shari Benstock argues that ALP keeps the letter in her vagina, thus putting her own inscription in a place HCE claims ("Nightletters" 230). Feminine language as undercurrent relates to Kristeva's semiotic, while Nut as the sky resembles Kristeva's idea of the *chora*, feminine receptive space (*Revolution* 24–29).

Works Cited

A Note on the *James Joyce Archive*

The *James Joyce Archive*, a series of reproductions of Joyce's manuscripts and notes, was published by Garland in New York in 1978 under the general editorship of Michael Groden. The sixty-three volumes were supposed to be numbered, but were not. A list of the numbers and the volumes that correspond to them appears in back of every issue of *James Joyce Quarterly*. I refer by number to the five volumes I cite, and follow the volume number with a period and the page number of the volume. Here are the numbers, the volumes they refer to, and their editors.

29 *Finnegans Wake: A Facsimile of Buffalo Notebooks VI.B.1–4.* Ed. David Hayman.

36 *Finnegans Wake: A Facsimile of Buffalo Notebooks VI.B.29–32.* Ed. Danis Rose.

40 *Finnegans Wake: A Facsimile of Buffalo Notebooks VI.B.45–50.* Ed. Danis Rose.

48 *Finnegans Wake: Book I, Chapter 8. A Facsimile of Drafts, Typescripts, and Proofs.* Ed. Danis Rose with John O'Hanlon. Prefaced by David Hayman.

63 *Finnegans Wake: Book IV. A Facsimile of Drafts, Typescripts, and Proofs.* Ed. Danis Rose with John O'Hanlon. Prefaced by David Hayman.

Acker, Kathy. *Blood and Guts in High School.* New York: Grove Press, 1978.

Alexander, Michael. *The Earliest English Poems: A Bilingual Edition.* Berkeley: U of California P, 1970.

Angelou, Maya. *Oh Pray My Wings Are Gonna Fit Me Well.* New York: Random House, 1975.

Atherton, James S. *The Books at the Wake: A Study of Literary Allusions. . . .* New York: Viking, 1960.

Attridge, Derek, ed. *The Cambridge Companion to James Joyce.* Cambridge: Cambridge UP, 1990.

Aubert, Jacques, ed. *Joyce avec Lacan.* Paris: Navarin Editeur, 1987.

Auden, W. H. *Selected Poems: New Edition.* Ed. Edward Mendelson. New York: Vintage, 1979.

Bakhtin, Mikhail M. *The Dialogic Imagination: Four Essays.* Trans. Caryl Emerson and Michael Holquist. Ed. Michael Holquist. Austin: U of Texas P, 1981.

Bal, Mieke. *Death and Dissymetry: The Politics of Coherence in the Book of Judges.* Chicago: U of Chicago P, 1988.

Bauerle, Ruth H., ed. *Picking Up Airs: Hearing the Music in Joyce's Text.* Urbana: U of Illinois P, 1993.

Bechet, Sidney. *Sidney Bechet and the New Orleans Feetwarmers,* Vol. 3. Joker SM 3573 (Milan), 1973.

Benstock, Bernard. *Joyce-again's Wake: An Analysis of* Finnegans Wake. Seattle: U of Washington P, 1965.

Benstock, Shari. "Nightletters: Woman's Writing in the *Wake.*" In *Critical Essays on James Joyce,* ed. Bernard Benstock. Boston: G. K. Hall, 1985.

Berg, Elizabeth L. "The Third Woman." *Diacritics* 12 (1982): 11–20.

Bhabha, Homi. *The Location of Culture.* London: Routledge, 1994.

Bishop, John. *Joyce's Book of the Dark:* Finnegans Wake. Madison: U of Wisconsin P, 1986.

Blake, William. *The Poetry and Prose of William Blake.* Ed. David V. Erdman. 2d ed. Garden City: Doubleday, 1970.

Bloom, Harold, and David Rosenberg. *The Book of J.* New York: Grove Weidenfeld, 1990.

Brewer, Ebenezer Cobham. *Brewer's Dictionary of Phrase and Fable.* Revised. New York: Harper and Bros., 1953.

Brivic, Sheldon. "The Femasculine Obsubject: A Lacanian Reading of FW 606–607." In *James Joyce's* Finnegans Wake: *A Casebook,* ed. John Harty III. New York: Garland, 1991.

Brivic, Sheldon. "Instinct in Tristania." *University of Hartford Studies in Literature* 12 (1980): 222-41.

Brivic, Sheldon. "Joyce between Genders: Lacanian Views." *James Joyce Quarterly* 29.1 (Fall 1991): 13–21. [Introduction to special issue of *JJQ* by this title that I edited with Ellie Ragland-Sullivan.]

Brivic, Sheldon. "The Terror and Pity of Love: ALP's Soliloquy." *James Joyce Quarterly* 29.1 (Fall 1991): 145–71.

Brivic, Sheldon. *The Veil of Signs: Joyce, Lacan, and Perception.* Urbana: U of Illinois P, 1991.

Brown, Norman O. *Life against Death: The Psychoanalytic Meaning of History.* Middletown: Wesleyan UP, 1959.

Brown, Richard. *James Joyce and Sexuality.* Cambridge: Cambridge UP, 1985.

Budge, E. A. Wallis. *The Book of the Dead: The Papyrus of Ani.* 1895. New York: Dover, 1967.

Butler, Samuel. *The Authoress of the* Odyssey: *Where and When She Wrote....* 1897, 1922. Chicago: U of Chicago P, 1967.

Campbell, Joseph, and Henry Morton Robinson. *A Skeleton Key to* Finnegans Wake. 1944. Harmondsworth: Penguin, 1977.

Card, James Van Dyck. *An Anatomy of "Penelope."* Madison, NJ: Fairleigh Dickinson UP, 1984.

Chart, David A. *The Story of Dublin*. Neudeln-Liechtenstein: Kraus Reprint, 1971.

Cheng, Vincent John. *Shakespeare and Joyce: A Study of* Finnegans Wake. University Park: Pennsylvania State UP, 1984.

Chodorow, Nancy J. *Feminism and Psychoanalytic Theory*. New Haven: Yale UP, 1989.

Cixous, Hélène. "Castration or Decapitation?" *Signs* 7.11 (1981): 41–55.

Cixous, Hélène. *The Exile of James Joyce*. Trans. Sally A. J. Purcell. New York: David Lewis, 1972.

Clément, Catherine. *The Lives and Legends of Jacques Lacan*. Trans. Arthur Goldhammer. New York: Columbia UP, 1983.

Deleuze, Gilles, and Félix Guattari. *Anti-Oedipus: Capitalism and Schizophrenia*. Trans. Robert Hurley et al. Minneapolis: U of Minnesota P, 1983.

Derrida, Jacques. *The Post Card: From Socrates to Freud and Beyond*. Trans. Alan Bass. Chicago: U of Chicago P, 1987.

Derrida, Jacques. "Two Words for Joyce." In *Post-Structuralist Joyce: Essays from the French*, ed. Derek Attridge and Daniel Ferrer. Cambridge: Cambridge UP, 1984.

Devlin, Kimberly J. "Castration and Its Discontents: A Lacanian Approach to *Ulysses.*" *James Joyce Quarterly* 29.1 (1991): 117–44.

Devlin, Kimberly J. "Pretending in 'Penelope': Masquerade, Mimicry, and Molly Bloom." *Novel* 25 (1991): 71–89.

Devlin, Kimberly J. "The Romance Heroine Exposed: 'Nausicaa' and *The Lamplighter.*" *James Joyce Quarterly* 22.4 (Summer 1985): 383–96.

Devlin, Kimberly J. *Wandering and Return in* Finnegans Wake: *An Integrative Approach to Joyce's Fictions*. Princeton: Princeton UP, 1991.

Dickie, Lois Galbraith. *No Respecter of Persons*. Pompano Beach, FL: Exposition Press, 1985.

Eagleton, Terry. *Literary Theory: An Introduction*. Minneapolis: U of Minnesota P, 1983.

Eckley, Grace. *Children's Lore in* Finnegans Wake. Syracuse: Syracuse UP, 1985.

Eckley, Grace. "Queer Mrs Quickenough and Odd Miss Doddpebble: The Tree and the Stone in *Finnegans Wake.*" In *Narrator and Character in* Finnegans Wake, by Michael H. Begnal and Grace Eckley. Lewisburg: Bucknell UP, 1975. 129–235.

Ellmann, Richard. *James Joyce*. Rev. ed. New York: Oxford UP, 1982.

Erdman, David V. *Blake: Prophet against Empire: A Poet's Interpretation of the History....* Rev. ed. Garden City: Doubleday, 1969.

Fast, Irene. *Gender Identity: A Differentiation Model*. Hillsdale, NJ: Analytic Press, 1984.

Felman, Shoshana. *What Does a Woman Want? Reading and Sexual Difference*. Baltimore: Johns Hopkins UP, 1993.

Flanagan, Thomas. *The Year of the French*. New York: Holt, Rinehart, and Winston, 1975.

Freud, Sigmund. *Moses and Monotheism*. Vol. 23 of *The Standard Edition of the Complete Psychological Works*. Trans. James Strachey and others. London: Hogarth, 1964. 1–138.

Freud, Sigmund. *The Question of Lay Analysis*. Vol. 20 of *The Standard Edition of the Complete Psychological Works*. Trans. James Strachey and others. London: Hogarth, 1959. 183–256.

Friedman, Susan Stanford, ed. *Joyce: The Return of the Repressed*. Ithaca: Cornell UP, 1993.

Frye, Northrop. "Quest and Cycle in *Finnegans Wake*." In *Fables of Identity: Studies in Poetic Mythology*. New York: Harcourt, Brace & World, 1963.

Gates, Henry Louis. *The Signifying Monkey: A Theory of Afro-American Literary Criticism*. New York: Oxford, 1988.

Gifford, Don, with Robert J. Seidman. *Ulysses Annotated: Notes for James Joyce's Ulysses*. Rev. ed. Berkeley: U of California P, 1988.

Gilbert, Sandra. "Life's Empty Pack: Notes toward a Literary Daughteronomy." *Critical Inquiry* 11 (1985): 355–84.

Gilbert, Sandra, and Susan Gubar. *No Man's Land*, Vol. 1: *The War of the Words: The Place of the Woman Writer*. . . . New Haven: Yale UP, 1987.

Gilman, Sander L. "Black Bodies, White Bodies: Toward an Iconography of Female Sexuality. . . ." In *"Race," Writing, and Difference*, ed. Henry Louis Gates, Jr. Chicago: U of Chicago P, 1986.

Girard, René. *Deceit, Desire, and the Novel: Self and Other in Literary Structure*. Trans. Yvonne Freccero. Baltimore: Johns Hopkins UP, 1966.

Glasheen, Adaline. *A Third Census of Finnegans Wake: An Index of the Characters and Their Roles*. Berkeley: U of California P, 1977.

Goldberg, Vicki. "In Search of Diana of Ephesus." *New York Times*, 21 Aug. 1994, H33.

Gordon, John. *Finnegans Wake: A Plot Summary*. Syracuse: Syracuse UP, 1986.

Gordon, John. "Love in Bloom, by Stephen Dedalus." *James Joyce Quarterly* 27.2 (Winter 1990): 241–55.

Gottfried von Strassburg. *Tristan* [German]. Ed. Reinhold Bechstein and Peter Ganz. Weisbaden: F. A. Brockhaus, 1978.

Gottfried von Strassburg. *Tristan*. Trans. A. T. Hatto. Harmondsworth: Penguin, 1960, 1967.

Grosz, Elizabeth. *Jacques Lacan: A Feminist Introduction*. London: Routledge, 1990.

Harrington, John P., ed. *Modern Irish Drama*. A Norton Critical Edition. New York: W. W. Norton, 1991.

Hart, Clive. *Structure and Motif in* Finnegans Wake. Evanston: Northwestern UP, 1962.

Hayman, David. *The "Wake" in Transit.* Ithaca: Cornell UP, 1990.

Henke, Suzette A. *James Joyce and the Politics of Desire.* New York: Routledge, 1990.

Herr, Cheryl. " 'Penelope' as Period Piece." *Novel* 22 (1989): 130–42.

Hill, Lynda M. "Hybridity and Boundariness: ALP's Ambivalent Offspring." Paper presented at XIV International James Joyce Symposium, Seville, June 1994.

Hurston, Zora Neale. *Their Eyes Were Watching God.* 1937. New York: Harper & Row, 1990.

Ions, Veronica. *Egyptian Mythology.* Rev. ed. New York: Peter Bedrick, 1983.

Irigaray, Luce. *This Sex Which is Not One.* Trans. Catherine Porter with Carolyn Burke. Ithaca: Cornell UP, 1985.

Jameson, Fredric. *The Political Unconscious: Narrative as a Socially Symbolic Act.* Ithaca: Cornell UP, 1981.

Joyce, James. *The Critical Writings of James Joyce.* Ed. Ellsworth Mason and Richard Ellmann. New York: Viking, 1959.

Joyce, James. *Dubliners.* Ed. Robert Scholes. New York: Viking, 1967.

Joyce, James. *Exiles.* New York: Viking, 1961.

Joyce, James. *Finnegans Wake.* 1939. New York: Viking, 1958.

Joyce, James. *James Joyce Reads.* Caedmon Cassette DCN 1340, remastered, 1992.

Joyce, James. *Letters of James Joyce.* Vol. 1. Ed. Stuart Gilbert. Rev. ed. New York: Viking, 1966.

Joyce, James. *Letters of James Joyce.* Vol. 2. Ed. Richard Ellmann. New York: Viking, 1966.

Joyce, James. *A Portrait of the Artist as a Young Man.* Case Studies in Contemporary Criticism. Ed. R. B. Kershner. New York: St. Martin's, 1993.

Joyce, James. *Selected Letters of James Joyce.* Ed. Richard Ellmann. New York: Viking, 1975.

Joyce, James. *Ulysses: The Corrected Text.* Ed. Hans Walter Gabler. New York: Vintage, 1986.

Kenner, Hugh. *Dublin's Joyce.* Bloomington: Indiana UP, 1956.

Kerenyi, Carl. *The Gods of the Greeks.* Trans. Norman Cameron. 1951. London: Thames and Hudson, 1974.

Kershner, R. B. *Joyce, Bakhtin, and Popular Literature: Chronicles of Disorder.* Chapel Hill: U of North Carolina P, 1989.

Knuth, Leo. "The Last Leaf." *A Wake Newslitter* 12 (1975): 103–7.

Kristeva, Julia. *Desire in Language: A Semiotic Approach to Literature and Art.* Trans. Thomas Gora and others. Ed. Leon S. Roudiez. New York: Columbia UP, 1980.

Kristeva, Julia. "Joyce 'The Gracehoper' or the Return of Orpheus." In *James*

Joyce: The Augmented Ninth, ed. Bernard Benstock. Syracuse: Syracuse UP, 1988.

Kristeva, Julia. *Revolution in Poetic Language*. Trans. Margaret Waller. New York: Columbia UP, 1984.

Kristeva, Julia. "Stabat Mater." In *The Kristeva Reader*, ed. Toril Moi. New York: Columbia UP, 1986. 160–86.

Lacan, Jacques. *Écrits: A Selection*. Trans. Alan Sheridan. New York: W. W. Norton, 1977.

Lacan, Jacques. *The Seminar of Jacques Lacan, Book I: Freud's Papers on Technique, 1953–1954*. Ed. Jacques-Alain Miller. Trans. John Forrester. New York: W. W. Norton, 1988.

Lacan, Jacques. *The Seminar of Jacques Lacan, Book VII: The Ethics of Psychoanalysis, 1959–1960*. Ed. Jacques-Alain Miller. Trans. Dennis Porter. New York: W. W. Norton, 1992.

Lacan, Jacques, and the *école freudienne*. *Feminine Sexuality*. Ed. Juliet Mitchell and Jacqueline Rose. Trans. Jacqueline Rose. New York: W. W. Norton, 1982.

Lemaire, Anika. *Jacques Lacan*. Trans. David Macey. London: Routledge and Kegan Paul, 1977.

Lennon, Florence Becker. *Lewis Carroll*. London: Cassell, 1947.

Lennon, John. *Live in New York City*. Capitol SV 12451, 1986.

Leonard, Garry M. *Reading* Dubliners *Again: A Lacanian Perspective*. Syracuse: Syracuse UP, 1993.

Levitt, Annette Shandler. "The Pattern out of the Wallpaper: Luce Irigaray and Molly Bloom." *Modern Fiction Studies* 35 (1989): 507–16.

Lewis, Walter "Furry." *Furry Lewis in His Prime, 1927–1928*. Yazoo 1050. No date on LP.

Lonnquist, Barbara. "Cannibalizing the Text: Isis and Rites of Allusion." Paper presented at XIV International James Joyce Symposium, Seville, June 1994.

Maddox, Brenda. *Nora: The Real Life of Molly Bloom*. Boston: Houghton Mifflin, 1988.

Mahaffey, Vicki. " 'Minxing marrage and making loof': Anti-Oedipal Reading." *James Joyce Quarterly* 30.2 (Winter 1993): 219–37.

Maitland, Margaret. *Life and Legends of St. Martin of Tours. (316–397)*. London: Catholic Truth Society, 1908.

Malory, Thomas. *The Works of Sir Thomas Malory*. Ed. Eugene Vinaver. London: Oxford, 1954.

Martin, Biddy. *Woman and Modernity: The (Life)Styles of Lou Andreas-Salome*. Ithaca: Cornell UP, 1991.

Martin, James D. *The Book of Judges: Commentary*. Cambridge: Cambridge UP, 1975.

Martin, Timothy. *Joyce and Wagner: A Study of Influence*. Cambridge: Cambridge UP, 1991.

Mascaro, Juan, trans. *The Upanishads*. Harmondsworth: Penguin, 1965.

McCarthy, Patrick A., ed. *Critical Essays on James Joyce's* Finnegans Wake. New York: G. K. Hall, 1992.

McGee, Patrick. *Telling the Other: The Question of Value in Modern and Postcolonial Writing*. Ithaca: Cornell UP, 1992.

McHugh, Roland. *Annotations to* Finnegans Wake. Rev. ed. Baltimore: Johns Hopkins UP, 1991.

McHugh, Roland. *The Sigla of* Finnegans Wake. Austin: U of Texas P, 1976.

Milesi, Laurent. "Metaphors of the Quest in *Finnegans Wake*." In Finnegans Wake: *Fifty Years*, European Joyce Studies 2, ed. Geert Lernout. Amsterdam and Atlanta: Rodopi, 1990.

Mill, John Stuart. *The Subjection of Women*. Ed. Susan Moller Okin. Indianapolis: Hackett, 1988.

Moi, Toril. *Sexual/Textual Politics: Feminist Literary Theory*. London: Methuen, 1985.

Montgomery, Niall. "The Pervigilium Phoenicis." *New Mexico Quarterly* 23 (1953): 437–72.

Moore, Kevin Z. Unpublished translation of "Joyce the Symptom II," by Jacques Lacan. [The French is in Aubert 31–36.]

Morrison, Toni. *Playing in the Dark: Whiteness and the Literary Imagination*. New York: Random House, 1992.

Nabokov, Vladimir. *Lolita*. New York: G. P. Putnam's Sons, 1955.

Nikhilananda, Swami. *The Upanishads*. Abridged ed. 1963. New York: Harper & Row, 1964.

Norris, Margot. *Joyce's Web: The Social Unravelling of Modernism*. Austin: U of Texas P, 1992.

Norris, Margot. "The Last Chapter of 'Finnegans Wake': Stephen Finds His Mother." *James Joyce Quarterly* 25.1 (Fall 1987): 11–30.

O'Dwyer, Riana. "Czarnowski and *Finnegans Wake*." *James Joyce Quarterly* 17.3 (Spring 1980): 281–91.

Olds, Sharon. *The Father*. New York: Knopf, 1993.

Opie, Iona, and Peter Opie, eds. *The Oxford Book of Nursery Rhymes*. London: Oxford, 1951, 1952.

Pearce, Richard. *The Politics of Narration: James Joyce, William Faulkner, and Virginia Woolf*. New Brunswick: Rutgers UP, 1991.

Polhemus, Robert M. "Dantellising Peaches and Miching Daddy, the Gushy Old Goof: The Browning Case. . . ." *Joyce Studies Annual* 1994:75–103.

Power, Arthur. *Conversations with James Joyce*. Ed. Clive Hart. New York: Harper & Row, 1974.

Rabaté, Jean-Michel. *Joyce upon the Void: The Genesis of Doubt*. New York: St. Martin's, 1991.

Ragland-Sullivan, Ellie. *Jacques Lacan and the Philosophy of Psychoanalysis*. Urbana: U of Illinois P, 1986.

Ragland-Sullivan, Ellie. "Psychosis Adumbrated: Lacan and the Sublimation of the Sexual Divide in Joyce's *Exiles*." *James Joyce Quarterly* 29.1 (Fall 1991): 47–62.

Reed, Ishmael. *Mumbo Jumbo*. New York: Bantam, 1973.

Riquelme, John Paul. *Teller and Tale in Joyce's Fiction: Oscillating Perspectives*. Baltimore: Johns Hopkins UP, 1983.

Rose, Danis, and John O'Hanlon. *Understanding* Finnegans Wake: *A Guide to the Narrative*. . . . New York: Garland, 1982.

Rougemont, Denis de. *Love in the Western World*. Trans. Montgomery Belgion. Rev. ed. New York: Pantheon, 1956.

Said, Edward W. *Culture and Imperialism*. New York: Vintage, 1994.

Sailer, Susan Shaw. *On the Void of to Be: Incoherence and Trope in* Finnegans Wake. Ann Arbor: U of Michigan P, 1993.

Scott, Bonnie Kime. *Joyce and Feminism*. Bloomington: Indiana UP, 1984.

Scott, Bonnie Kime. *James Joyce*. Feminist Readings Series. Atlantic Highlands, NJ: Humanities Press International, 1987.

Senn, Fritz. "Every Klitty of a scolderymeid: Sexual-Political Analogies." *A Wake Newslitter* 3 (1962): 1–7.

Shakespeare, William. *Hamlet*. Arden Edition. Ed. Harold Jenkins. London: Methuen, 1982.

Shakespeare, William. *The Riverside Shakespeare*. Ed. G. Blakemore Evans and others. Boston: Houghton Mifflin, 1974.

Shechner, Mark. *Joyce in Nighttown: A Psychoanalytic Inquiry into Ulysses*. Berkeley: U of California P, 1974.

Showalter, Elaine. "Feminist Criticism in the Wilderness." *Critical Inquiry* 8 (1981): 243–70.

Skeat, Walter W. *A Concise Etymological Dictionary of the English Language*. New York: Harper and Bros., 1882.

Solomon, Margaret. *Eternal Geomater: The Sexual Universe of* Finnegans Wake. Carbondale: Southern Illinois UP, 1969.

Sophocles. *Sophocles I: Oedipus the King, Oedipus at Colonus, Antigone*. Ed. David Grene and Richmond Lattimore. *Antigone*, trans. Elizabeth Wyckoff. New York: Washington Square, 1967.

Storey, Robert F. " 'I Am I Because My Little Dog Knows Me': Prolegomenon. . . ." *Criticism* 32 (1990): 419–48.

Strean, Herbert S. *The Sexual Dimension: A Guide for the Helping Professional*. New York: Free Press, 1983.

Troy, William. "Notes on *Finnegans Wake*." In *James Joyce: Two Decades of Criticism*, ed. Seon Givens. New York: Vanguard Press, 1948, 1963.

Upanishads. *See* Mascaro and Nikhilananda.

Van Mierlo, Wim. "St. Martin of Tours in VI.B.2." Forthcoming in *A Finnegans Wake Circular*.

Velikovsky, Immanuel. *Oedipus and Akhnaton: Myth and History*. Garden City: Doubleday, 1960.

Warner, Marina. "More than Friendship." *New York Times Book Review*, 28 Aug. 1994, 7–8.

Winnicott, D. W. *Playing and Reality*. Harmondsworth: Penguin, 1974.

Yeats, William Butler. *The Poems: A New Edition*. Ed. Richard J. Finneran. New York: Macmillan, 1983.

Žižek, Slavoj. *The Sublime Object of Ideology*. London: Verso, 1989.

Index

Titles by Joyce, Lacan, and Shakespeare are listed under the author, except for *Finnegans Wake*.

Acker, Kathy, 93
Adam, 79, 110
Adultery, 40, 68, 77
Aeneas, 94
Africa, 24, 31, 51, 54–67, 94
"Africa" (Angelou), 62–63
Akhnaton, 142*n*3
Albert Nyanza (lake), 60
Alexander, Michael, 96
Alexander the Great, 94
ALP (Anna Livia Plurabelle): as ur-subject of this book, x; initial definition of, 5–6; resolving male conflict, 17; creates men, 18–19, 90, 92–93, 99–101, 108, 128; attacks patriarchy, 23–24, 27, 76, 85, 108–10; between opposites, 23–24, 36–37; assumes narrative, 23–25, 132, 134–35; as letter writer, 24, 83–89, 99–100; fused with Issy, 24, 89, 126, 129; as flux, 35–67; as product of gossip, 37–38; compromised by men, 39–41, 101–4, 107; childhood of, under virginity taboo, 41–44; lost gifts and messages of, 44–46, 100; as deity, 52; as Africa, 54–67, 94; youth of, among women, 55, 118; as Nile source, 60; as mother, 75, 126; as tragic, 82–83, 117–23, 134; and her father, 102–4; self-realization of, 108, 113, 123; rejects Symbolic, 108, 117; returns to mother, 126–31
Amazons, 109, 130
Anagram, 71, 75

Anapests, 130
Angelou, Maya, 62–63
Ankhnesneferibre, 127
Anna (in the *Aeneid*), 94
Anna Livia Plurabelle (pamphlet), 55–56. See ALP (Anna Livia Plurabelle) *for character*
Antigone, 25, 83, 117, 119–23, 125, 128, 134
Antony (Mark), 95–96
Aristotle, 106, 122
Arklow, Michael, 41–42, 65
Armstrong, Louis, 63
Arthur, King, 91, 99
Arrah-na-Pogue, 115
"As I was Going to St. Ives" (riddle), 45, 51
Asia, 62, 66
Atherton, James S., 67
Attridge, Derek, 4, 139*n*4, 140*ch*2*n*2
Aubert, Jacques, 9, 139*n*4
Auden, W. H., 81
Awakening, The (Chopin), 119

Bach, Johann Sebastian, 76–77
Bakhtin, Mikhail M., 39
Bal, Mieke, 27
Balfe, Michael, 32
Barak, 28
Bauerle, Ruth H., 63
Beauty, 118–21
Bechet, Sidney, 65
Beckman, Richard, 142*n*9

Bédier, 75
Bees, 30, 33
Benstock, Bernard, 71, 128
Benstock, Shari, 3, 143n4
Berg, Elizabeth L., 21
Bhabha, Homi, 54
Bible, 27–31, 56, 74, 86, 90
Biddy. *See* Doran, Biddy (hen); O'Brien,
    Biddy
Birds, 31–34, 76, 116, 124, 125–26, 128
Bisexuality, 18, 51–52, 72–74, 78, 109, 133
Bishop, John, ix, 3, 4, 19, 126
Blake, William, 32, 62, 77
Bloom, David, 120
Bloom, Harold, 28
Bloom, Leopold, 7–8, 16, 18, 40, 47, 49,
    82, 91, 118, 119, 125, 130
Bloom, Milly, 118
Bloom, Molly, 3, 7–8, 13, 15, 18, 57, 62,
    118
Book of Judges, 28–29
Boswell, John, 141ch5n4
Boucicault, Dion, 115
Boylan, Blazes, 7–8, 13, 82, 110
Breasts, 52, 130. *See also* Nursing
Breen, Josie, 118
Brewer, Ebenezer, 142n7
Brivic, Barbara, 52, 94, 96, 141n7
Brivic, Sheldon, ix, 52, 70, 140n10
Brontë, Emily, 134
Brown, Norman O, 61
Brown, Richard, 79
Bruno, Giordano, 18, 23, 134
Buckley, 14
Budge, E. A. Wallis, 126
Burn, Barefoot, 42
Burns, Robert, 32
Butler, Samuel, 27

Campbell, Joseph, 139n8, 141ch4n3
Campion, Jane, 15
Card, James Van Dyck, 7
Carroll, Lewis, 91
Cartland, Barbara, 15
Cave of Lovers, 75–77, 98
Chapel, 71–78, 83, 98–99, 116, 124, 129
Chapelizod, 74, 83

Chart, David A., 74
Chaucer, Geoffrey, 77
Cheng, Vincent John, 93, 94
Chodorow, Nancy, 37, 90, 117–18
Chopin, Kate, 119
Christ, 73, 100
Cixous, Hélène, 6, 41, 62, 125–26, 139n3
Clarence, duke of, Albert Victor, 32
Clément, Catherine, 142n12
Cleopatra, 93–96
Clery, Emma, 9, 41
Coffin, Justin, 5
Coleridge, Samuel Taylor, 41, 58–59
Colonialism, 48, 63, 107–8, 115
Columbus, Rualdus, 14
Columella, 28
Conan, 110
"The Congo" (Lindsay), 57
Conrad, Joseph, 67
Conroy, Gabriel, 17, 85
Conroy, Gretta, 9, 17, 85, 96
Creon, 117, 119, 121–22
Czarnowski, Stefan, 121

Daedalus, 115
Davis, Martha, 142n10
Deborah, 27–31, 76
Deconstruction, 4, 27
Dedalus, May, 9, 125
Dedalus, Stephen, 9, 10, 16, 17, 34, 82, 99,
    111
Deleuze, Gilles, 121
Derrida, Jacques, 6, 84, 139n4
Devlin, Kimberly, 3, 8, 9, 98, 111, 139n5
Diana, Princess, 40
Diana of Ephesus, 32–33, 61
Dickie, Lois Galbraith, 27
Dido, 94
Dillon, Floey, 118
Dodpebble, Miss, 35–37, 44–50, 61, 66, 105
A Doll's House (Ibsen), 10
Dolph (Shem), 128
Doran, Biddy (hen), 5, 46, 124
Doyle, Arthur Conan, 110
Dryden, John, 41, 48
Dual-gender pronouns, 46, 140n3
Dublin, 102, 108, 117

The Duchess of Malfi (Webster), 122

Eagleton, Terry, 21
Earwicker, Humphrey Chimpden. *See* HCE (Humphrey Chimpden Earwicker)
Eckley, Grace, 27, 35
Écriture féminine. See Feminine writing
Egyptian myth, 25, 52, 126–29, 142*n*3
Ellmann, Richard, 4, 11, 17, 26 43–44, 63, 113, 115
Emerson, Ralph Waldo, 20
Erdman, David, 62
Evangelists (four), 48, 90
Eve, 5, 49, 79

Fast, Irene, 21
Father, 42, 111, 114, 118, 142*n*12
Father Ocean, 111, 113
Faulkner, William, 15, 48, 67
Felman, Shoshana, 5
Femasculine obsubject, 70–71, 133
Feminine writing, 6–7, 22, 55, 110
Feminism: problems of male feminists, 3–4, 8–9, 14; deconstructive role of, 4, 27, 121; and social criticism vs. feminine writing, 6–7; and gender polarity, 19, 22; and essentialism, 21; American vs. French, 22–23; and problem of power, 109; position of, in the *Wake*, 132–34. *See also* Chodorow, Nancy; Cixous, Hélène; Gilbert, Sandra; Grosz, Elizabeth; Irigaray, Luce; Kristeva, Julia; Mill, John Stuart; Showalter, Elaine
Finn. *See* MacCool, Finn
Finnegans Wake, by chapter (*see* 139*n*7): I.1, 23–24, 57, 60–61, 67; I.2, 67, 86; I.4, 38–39, 57; I.5 (Letter), 41, 84, 128; I.6 (Questions), 20, 56, 69, 75; I.7 (Shem), 10, 35, 56, 59, 67; I.8, (ALP), 11, 32, 35–67, 72–3, 124; II.1 (Games), 12–14, 58, 75, 77; II.2 (Lesson), 20, 32, 57, 128; II.3 (Tavern), 31, 33, 70, 92, 125, 130; II.4 (Ship), 77–78; III.2, 20; III.3, 56, 77; III.4 (Bed), 56, 88, 97, 100, 101; IV, 11, 65–66, 69, 81–131

Flanagan, Anne-Marie, 42
Flanagan, Thomas, 142*n*5
Flaubert, Gustave, 58, 119
Freud, Sigmund, 5, 18, 39, 42, 52, 56, 103, 142*n*3
Friedman, Susan Stanford, 7, 15
Frigidity, 107
Froula, Christine, 15
Frye, Northrop, 11
Furey, Michael, 41

Gates, Henry Louis, 65
Genet, Jean, 93
Ghirlandaio, Domenico, 71
Gideon, 140*ch*2*n*1
Gifford, Don, 14, 57, 72, 124–25
Gilbert, Sandra, 22, 42, 103, 120
Gilman, Sander L., 56
Girard, René, 88
Glasheen, Adeline, 32, 46, 60, 73, 93, 115, 140*ch*2*n*1
Goldberg, Vicki, 33
"Goodbye" (song), 57
Goosing, 104, 109–10
Gordon, John, 16, 36, 102
Gossip, 37–41
Gottfried von Strassburg, 75–77, 98
El Greco, 71
Gregory, Lady, 50
Gripes, 56
Grosz, Elizabeth, 4, 26, 114
Guattari, Felix, 121
Gubar, Susan, 22

Harrington, John P., 50
Hart, Clive, 27, 28, 84
Hayman, David, 24, 76
HCE (Humphrey Chimpden Earwicker): as male principle, 4; as bound to fall, 16, 67, 70; frightens children, 29; as unfaithful, 39, 45; molests ALP, 39, 51–52, 93, 102–5; ALP promotes, 44, 84–93, 97–100; as dreamer, 46; women long for, 48–49; as imperialist, 51, 107; bisexuality and, 51–52, 72–74; as Nile source, 60; mixed in marriage, 68–71; as product of ALP, 83, 92, 100;

HCE (*continued*)
    imagined by ALP, 97–107; as
    incestuous, 102–7; ALP rejects, 107,
    109, 126, 130–31; ALP attacks, 108–10;
    supports ALP, 114–15
Hegel, Georg W. F., 16
Heliotrope, 31, 58
Henke, Suzette, 3, 15, 44, 52, 91, 92, 97
Henri, IV, 140*ch3n1*
Herman, Judith Lewis, 103
Herodotus, 83
Herr, Cheryl, 139*n5*
Hilary (twin), 23–24
Hill, Lynda, 54, 56
Hoang Ho (river), 53
Homer, 27, 76
Homosexuality (male), 14, 41, 51,
    73–74
Horus, 128
Howth, Hill of, 89, 99, 118
Hurston, Zora Neale, 87

Ibsen, Henrik, 3, 10, 14, 26, 96, 119
"I Dreamt that I Dwelt" (song), 32
Imaginary order, 6, 43
Imperialism, 14, 48, 51, 60
Incest, 102–4, 120, 142*n8*
Ions, Veronica, 43, 126
Ireland, 28, 100, 107–8
Irish dialect, 126
Irish myth, 4, 46, 121. *See also* Isolde;
    Tristan
Irigaray, Luce: and women's point of
    view, 4; and dispersed view of women,
    6, 7, 8, 97; pleasure of women: 19, 31,
    43; critique of, 21; against male
    thinkers, 22, 26, 42, 84; on women as
    unknown, 60, 63, 70, 74; and the other
    side perspective, 67; on women
    reflecting men, 81, 98; on repressed
    woman's body, 99, 133; on feminine
    mechanics of fluids, 119–120, 130; on
    Antigone, 122; on the sky, 129; on
    masquerade, 139*n5*
"I saw a chapel off of gold" (Blake), 77
Isis, 52, 126
Ismene, 121

Isolde (Isode, Isot, Izod), 36, 74–75, 76,
    78, 83, 98
Issy (Isabel, Isolde), joined to ALP, 5, 24,
    126; militant feminism of, 11–15;
    aggression of, 19–20; as singer, 31–34;
    African descent of, 58; as mother's
    beauty, 74; behavior of, to avoid rape,
    76; replacing mother, 88–89, 126;
    linked to sky, 128–29

Jael, 28–29
James Joyce. See Ellmann, Richard
Jameson, Fredric, 37, 123
Jarl van Hoother, 23, 27
Jonson, Ben, 128
Joyce, Eileen, 43
Joyce, Giorgio, 115
Joyce, James: overcame traditional
    background, 3; attacked patriarchy, 6;
    developed feminine language, 6–7;
    sexist humor of, 8–9, 14; wrote for
    women, 9–10; aiming at women (four
    ways), 9–10, 15–16; increasing
    feminism of, 11, 124; appropriating
    women, 14–15; need of, to be rejected,
    15–17, 133; regarded masculinity as
    wound, 17–18, idea of, that genders
    create each other, 18–19; valued
    feminine changefulness, 23; on
    incestuous desire, 103; idea of, that
    love seeks impossible, 112; need of, to
    free women, 115; skepticism of, 124; on
    feminism in dialectic, 134
—works: "Araby," 6, 16; *Archive*, 24, 39,
    43, 73, 89, 102, 111, 115, 124; "Clay",
    6, 32; "Counterparts," 6; *Critical
    Writings*, 3, 14, 26, 119; "The Dead," 9,
    17, 31, 85, 96; *Dubliners*, 6, 9, 17, 31, 32,
    72, 85, 96; "Eveline," 6; *Exiles*, 16, 40,
    112; "Grace," 6; *Joyce Reads*, 47, 52, 70;
    Letters, 9, 10, 12, 14, 44–45, 123; "A
    Painful Case," 6; *A Portrait of the
    Artist*, 9, 10, 16, 17, 18, 41, 42, 46, 82,
    99, 111, 115; "Two Gallants," 72;
    Ulysses, 7–8, 9, 10, 14, 16, 17, 18, 20,
    34, 40, 42, 46, 47, 49, 57, 63, 72, 82, 90,
    119, 121. *See also Finnegans Wake*

Joyce, Lucia, 63, 103, 115
Joyce, Mary, 9–10, 113, 139*n6*
Joyce, Nora Barnacle, 9, 14, 43–44, 101, 113, 117, 118
Joyce, Stanislaus, 17, 139*n6*

Kallisto, 33
Kate, 5, 36, 46, 51, 53. *See also* Dodpebble, Miss; Quickenough, Mrs.
Katha Upanishad, 66–67
Kennedy, Jacqueline, 40
Kenner, Hugh, 112
Kerenyi, Carl, 33
Kermode, Frank, 96
Kernan, Mrs., 6
Kev (Shaun), 128
Kiswahili, 55, 61, 65
"Knocked 'em in the Old Kent Road" (song), 31
Knuth, Leo, 94
Koyana, Siphokazi, 65
Kristeva, Julia, 6, 29, 47, 70, 114, 139*n3*
"Kubla Khan" (Coleridge), 58–59

Lacan, Jacques: ambiguous feminism of, 3–4, 22; on Joyce, 6, 9, 139*n4*; critique of masculinity by, 17, 18, 92; on the phallus, 18, 95; on tragedy, 25, 105, 117–22; on woman's *jouissance*, 32, 89; on the Other, 69, 78, 98; on self-division, 72, 81–84; on the Thing, 99, 120; on incest, 103; on the law of the father, 111; on love, 112. *See* Imaginary order; Other; Symbolic order
—works: *Écrits*, 69; *Encore*: 22; *Ethnics of Psychoanalysis*, 25, 72, 99, 105, 117–22; *Feminine Sexuality*, 18, 82, 89, 92, 98; *Freud's Papers on Technique*, 112; *Joyce avec Lacan*, 9, 84; "Joyce the Symptom II," 84
Laertes, 42
Lane, Lois, 115
Law of the father, 111, 122
Lawrence, D. H., 67
Leda, 115
Leeds, Nina, 40
Lemaire, Anika, 98

Lennon, Florence, 91
Lennon, John, 63
Lesbianism, 14, 50, 61, 109, 112, 118
Levitt, Annette Shandler, 139*n1*
Levitt, Morton, 141*ch6n2*
Lewis, Walter "Furry", 63
Life Against Death (Brown), 61
Liffey river, 4, 24, 102, 113
Lindsay, Vachel, 57, 140*ch4n2*
Lolita (Nabokov), 104
Lonnquist, Barbara, 56
Luke (Gospel), 13
Lysistrata, 121

McAlmon, Robert, 63
McCarthy, Patrick, 84
MacCool, Finn, 4, 106, 112
MacDowell, Gerty, 33, 47, 63
McGee, Patrick, 19, 20
McHugh, Roland: 13, 20, 28, 29, 32, 33, 34, 41, 45, 46, 49, 52, 56, 61, 65, 66, 69, 80, 85, 86, 93, 97, 100, 101, 102, 106, 109, 114, 125, 128, 129, 139*n9*
Maddox, Brenda, 8–9, 10–11, 118
Maggy (or Maggies), 33, 84, 86, 129
Magrath, 86–88, 109–110
Mahaffey, Vicki, 141*ch5n1*
Maitland, Margaret, 73–74
Malory, Sir Thomas, 75
Menanaan, 85
Mark, King, 76
Marriage, 60, 68–71, 75–80
Marriage of Heaven and Hell (Blake), 62
Martin, Biddy, 20
Martin, James, 27
Martin, Timothy, 32, 52, 76
Martini, Simone, 71
Marvell, Andrew, 106
Mascaro, Juan, 66
Masculinity, 18, 87, 108
Maternal space, 78, 120, 124, 129–30
Matriarchy, 28, 126, 133
Melnicoff, Roz; 142*n2*
Mercier, Vivian, 60
Michael, Father, 41
Milesi, Laurent, 60–61, 74
Mill, John Stuart, 60, 93, 132

Milton, John, 48, 79–80, 105
Mitchell, Juliet, 4
Moi, Toril, 23, 125
Montgomery, Niall, 71
Mookse, 56
Moore, Kevin Z., 141*ch6n1*
Moran, Father, 41
Morrison, Toni, 55, 63, 65
Mother, 75, 116–17, 125, 126, 128
Motifs, 26–27
Mulligan, Buck, 17, 18
Murdock, George Peter, 40

Nabokov, Vladimir, 104
Naughtingels, song of, 31, 128
Nietzsche, Friedrich, 20
Nikhilinanda, Swami, 67
Nora: The Real Life of Molly Bloom. See
  Maddox, Brenda
Norris, Margot, 3, 11, 36–37, 141*ch6n4*
Norwegian Captain, 129
Nursing, 51–52, 95
Nut (goddess), 25, 43, 63, 117, 126–29

O'Brien, Biddy, 46
O'Connor, Roderick, 100
O'Dwyer, Riana, 121
Oedipus, 117, 120, 128
Oenone, 38–39
Ogden, C. K., 46, 49
O'Hanlon, John, 31, 61, 110
Olds, Sharon, 50
O'Malley, Grace, 24
O'Neill, Eugene, 40
Ono, Yoko, 63
Ophelia, 42, 119
Opie, Iona and Peter, 45
O'Reilly, Persse, 86
Osiris, 126
Other: 59, 63, 66, 68–69, 78, 80, 82, 90, 98,
  111, 112, 120–21
Ovid, 142*n10*

Pandora: 44
Paradise Lost, 79, 104–5
Paris (hero), 38–39
Paris (city), 7, 139*n3*

Patriarchy, 6, 14, 27, 100, 110, 113–14,
  121, 132, 133
Pearce, Richard, 5
Pepi II, 128
Phallus, 4, 16, 18, 51, 87, 92–93, 100, 108
Pliny, 28
Plurabelle, Anna Livia. *See* ALP (Anna
  Livia Plurabelle)
Plutarch, 129
Polhemus, Robert, 103
Pontellier, Edna, 119
Power, Arthur, 10
Prankquean, 23, 27
Prometheus Unbound (Shelley), 30, 62
Prostitution, 12, 17, 48
Purcell, Henry, 94

The Question of Lay Analysis (Freud), 56
Quickenough, Mrs., 35–37, 44–5, 105
Quinet, Edgar, 28, 119

Rabaté, Jean Michel, 70, 140*n4*
Ragland-Sullivan, Ellie, 98
Rape, 30, 39, 48, 76
Reed, Ishmael, 140*ch4n2*
Reynard, 39
Rhea, 129
Rhythm, 29, 130
Richardson, Dorothy, 6
Riquelme, John Paul, ix
"The Rising of the Moon," 50
Robin, 124, 129
Robinson Crusoe, 124
Robinson, Henry Morton, 139*n8*,
  141*ch4n3*
Rose, Danis, 31, 61, 110
"A Rose for Emily," 48
Rose, Jacqueline, 98
de Rougemont, Denis, 76
Rowan, Richard, 16, 112
Rubek, Arnold, 26

Sacher-Masoch, Leopold von, 110
Sade, Marquis de, 121
Said, Edward, 125
Saint Bernard, 47
Saint Bridget, (Brigid), 46, 99

Saint Martin, 33, 71–74
Saint Mary, 12–13, 47, 101, 129
Saint Patrick, 52
Saint Paul, 30
Sailer, Susan Shaw, 3, 4, 58
Sappho, 15, 61
Scott, Bonnie Kime, 3, 11, 19, 126, 140n12
Schneider, Ulrich, 125
Seb, 126
Seidman, Robert J., 14, 57, 72, 124–25
Semiotic, 110, 132
Senn, Fritz, 13
Shakespeare, William: 17, 42, 82, 90,
    93–96, 115, 118, 119, 120–21
—plays: Antony and Cleopatra, 93–96;
    Hamlet, 42, 90, 93, 119, 120–21; King
    Lear, 93, 115, 118; Macbeth, 93; Othello,
    93; Romeo and Juliet, 93
Shaun, 14, 20, 31–32, 33, 42, 66, 128, 129
Sheba, Queen of, 58
Shechner, Mark, 9
Sheela-na-gig, 44
Shelley, 30, 62
Shem, 20, 59, 66, 128
Showalter, Elaine, 6, 7, 28
Sigla, 19, 111
Signifier, 90, 99–100, 111
Sisera, 28–30
Skeat, Walter W., 37, 48, 91
Sky, 25, 67, 126, 128, 129
Sleeping Beauty, 100
Solomon, Margaret, 99
Song, 27–34, 43, 59, 76, 116, 124, 125, 128
Song of Dawn, 31–34, 125, 129, 130, 134
Sophocles, 3, 117–23
Spengler, Oswald, 65, 141ch4n3
Stanhope, Hester, 118
Stedman, Capt. J. G., 62
Stein, Gertrude, 7, 67
Sterne, Laurence, 20, 34
Storey, Robert, 40
Strange Interlude (O'Neill), 40
Strean, Herbert S., 140ch3n2
Sublime object, 16, 133
Sully, 106
Superman, 115
Swift, Jonathan, 20, 72–73

"Swing Low, Sweet Chariot" (song), 31
Symbolic order, 43, 81, 100, 118, 120, 121,
    122, 123, 125, 132, 134

A Tale of a Tub (Swift), 72–73
Tate, Nahum, 94
Tennyson, Lord Alfred, 37, 38
Their Eyes were Watching God (Hurston),
    87
Thing, 120, 122, 124
Third World, 54, 62, 67, 125
This Sex Which Is Not One. See Irigaray,
    Luce
"To his Coy Mistress" (Marvell), 106
Toussaint, Rhonda, 12
Tragedy, 82, 83, 117–23, 134
Tree and stone, 51, 134
Tristan (Tristram, Trystram), 74, 75–78,
    98, 123
Tristan (Gottfried), 75, 76, 77, 98
Tristan und Isolde (Wagner), 76
Tristopher (twin), 23–24
Tristram Shandy, 34
Troy, William, 130

"Under-wood," 128
Upanishads, 66–67

Van Mierlo, Wim, 73, 141ch5n3
Velikovsky, Immanuel, 142n3
Venus in Furs (Sacher-Masoch), 110
Vicocyclometer, 37, 38, 83
Victoria Nyanza (lake), 60
Vikings, 107–8
Virag, Lipoti, 14
Virgil, 94
Visions of the Daughters of Albion (Blake),
    62

Wade, Wallowme, 42
Wagner, Richard, 52–53
Warner, Marina, 141ch5n4
Washerwomen, 32, 35–39, 41, 44, 47, 49,
    66, 83
Water, 35–36, 38, 109, 129–31
Weaver, Harriet Shaw, 9, 11, 12, 44, 60
Webster, John, 3, 122

"When the Red Red Robin Comes Bob
Bob Bobbin Along" (song), 124, 142*n2*
When We Dead Awaken (Ibsen), 26
"The Wild Man of Borneo" (song),
124–25, 130
"The Wife's Lament" (lyric), 96
Winnicott, D. W., 78, 114
Woman as Colonized. *See* Colonialism
"Woman is the Nigger of the World"
(song), 63

Woods, Harry, 124
Woolf, Virginia, 6, 67, 134
"Wulf and Eadwacer," 96

X, Malcolm, 55

Yared, Aïda, 39, 48, 134
Yeats, William Butler, 49, 58, 119–20

Žižek, Slavoj, 16, 120–21, 123, 133